Charlie Brown's Third Super Book of Questions and Answers

...about all kinds of boats and planes, cars and trains and other things that move!

Charlie Brown's Third Super Book of Questions and Answers

...about all kinds of boats and planes
cars and trains and other things that move!

Based on the Charles M. Schulz Characters

Random House New York

Art Director: Eleanor Ehrhardt
Designer: Terry Flanagan
Layout: Charlotte Staub
Picture Research: Anne Christensen
Production Director: Edward McGill
Editor: Hedda Nussbaum

Special thanks to:
Dr. Ira Freeman
Professor of Physics
Rutgers University

Photograph and Illustration Credits: Bryan and Cherry Alexander/Bruce Coleman, Inc., 3; American Airlines, 120, 138, 139; American Hall of Aviation History, Northrop University, 102, 103, 117; American Museum of Natural History, 4; American Trucking Associations, Inc., 40, 41; Association of American Railroads, 30, 31; Capt. Bartlett/American Museum of Natural History, 53; British Airways, 129; James J. Cariello, 20; Cessna Aircraft Company, 125, 126; John M. Christensen, 41, 81; Henning Christoph/Black Star, 37; Copyright 1978 The Cousteau Society, Inc., 87, 93; Cunard Line, 70, 71; Danish Tourist Board, 90; Peter Dickerson/Editorial Photocolor Archives, 107; Editorial Photocolor Archives, 110; Eleanor Ehrhardt, 36, 75, 84, 85, 124, 136; Giorgio Gualco/Bruce Coleman, Inc., 3, 51; Indianapolis Motor Speedway Corporation, 24; Kennebec Valley Chamber of Commerce/Paul Fournier, 46, 135; McAllister Brothers, Inc., 77; McDonnell Douglas Corporation, 134; Ed McGill, 79, 81; The Metropolitan Museum of Art, Rogers Fund, 1903, 6; The Metropolitan Museum of Art Excavations, 1919-20; Rogers Fund, Supplemented by Contribution of Edward S. Harkness, 55; Missouri Historical Society, 67; Moran Inland Waterways Corporation, 75; National Aeronautics and Space Administration, 25, 141, 142; National Automotive History Collection, Detroit Public Library, 18, 20; National Oceanic and Atmospheric Administration, National Ocean Survey, 88; Newell and Adlington/American Museum of Natural History, 3; New York City Fire Department Photo Unit, 42, 43, 76, 78, 133; The New York Historical Society, 68; New York State Department of Commerce, 3, 28, 47, 101, 106; Norwegian Information Service, 50; Nova Scotia Communications and Information Centre, 63, 91; Walter T. Otto, Jr., 83; Plimoth Plantation, Plymouth, Massachusetts, 62; San Francisco Visitors Bureau, 27; Shor/American Museum of Natural History, 3; Sikorsky Aircraft Division of United Technologies, 132; Smithsonian Institution, National Air and Space Museum, 98, 109, 113, 114; Kenneth H. Stauffer, 17; I.N. Phelps Stokes Collection, Prints Division, The New York Public Library, Astor, Lenox and Tilden Foundation, 66; Swedish Information Service, 57; U.S. Air Force, 108, 113, 116, 130, 131; U.S. Navy, 92, 94, 95, 96; United States Virgin Islands, 81.

Library of Congress Cataloging in Publication Data

Main entry under title: Charlie Brown's third super book of questions and answers...about all kinds of boats and planes, cars and trains and other things that move! SUMMARY: Charlie Brown and the rest of the Peanuts gang help present a host of facts about various modes of transportation in a question and answer format. 1. Transportation—Juvenile literature. 2. Transportation—Miscellanea. [1. Transportation. 2. Questions and answers.] I. Title.
HE243.S35   380.5   78-7404
ISBN 0-394-83729-0   ISBN 0-394-93729-5 lib. bdg.

Manufactured in the United States of America

1 2 3 4 5 6 7 8 9

Introduction

Have you ever wondered who invented the wheel? Or why cars have license plates? Or how a submarine goes up and down? Or how a heavy airplane can stay up in the air? If you have, you've come to the right book. It will give you the answers to all these questions and to many, many others—about all kinds of boats and planes, cars and trains, buses, helicopters, sleds, and other things that move.

Once again Charlie Brown, Snoopy, Lucy, Sally, Peppermint Patty, Linus, Woodstock, and the rest of the Peanuts gang are here to help out with the answers. So join them and start asking the questions!

Contents

CHOP
CHOP
CHOP
CHOP
CHOP

Charlie Brown on Land

How did people first travel?

They walked. Before people knew of any other way to travel, they used what nature gave them to move from one place to another—their feet. But foot travel was slow. When people wanted to go long distances, they had to spend weeks, months, or even years.

1

Why did people use animals for travel?

Large animals such as mules and camels are strong enough to carry people on their backs. And they don't tire as quickly as people. So when men, women, and children started to ride animals, they were able to travel long distances more quickly than before. They were also able to get to where they were going without becoming so tired.

How did people first carry things?

People first carried things in their arms and on their backs—and they still do. They also balance things on their heads. But arms, backs, and heads can carry only lightweight loads. People quickly tire from their burdens. So about 8,000 years ago, they began to tame animals to carry things.

What animals have people used to carry things?

People have used whatever strong, easy-to-tame animals they have found living in their lands. And they still use these "beasts of burden" for carrying things and for pulling carts, wagons, and sleds. In the desert lands of Egypt and Syria people use oxen, donkeys, and camels. Camels are especially good for desert travel. Deserts are dry. Camels can go for long periods without water. Reindeer are ideal for the people of icy Lapland. Reindeer move quickly in snow and can carry up to 300 pounds. Llamas are good mountain climbers. They carry things for the Indians of Peru in the Andes Mountains. The people of ancient Iran were the first to tame horses. Horses can move faster for a longer period of time than all other animals. In India elephants carry loads on their backs and even in their trunks. Eskimos near the North Pole train dogs to pull sleds and carry light loads.

Reindeer

Indian elephant

Camel

Donkey

Dog sled team

Llamas

What did the American Indians use to carry supplies?

Many American Indians used the travois (truh-VOY) to carry things. It was made of two long poles. The front or middle of the poles was attached to an animal. The bottom end dragged along the ground. The Indians strapped their supplies to the poles. For many years they used a dog to pull the travois. But after European settlers brought horses to America, the Indians used a horse instead.

How did Roman emperors travel?

The emperors and the rich people of Rome were carried on litters. A litter is a couch on two poles. Four slaves carried it on their shoulders. While the slaves walked with their load, the passenger lounged on the couch. There were so many litters that they caused real traffic jams in ancient Rome.

Did people ever use sleds without snow?

Yes, they did, and they still do. The sledge was one of the earliest vehicles—objects that carry people or things from one place to another. At first a sledge was just a flat piece of wood, dragged along the ground. Then people added wooden runners to it. These were much like the metal runners on a modern snow sled. Oxen, and possibly other animals, pulled the sledges.

What good were sledges?

Early people found that an object moved along the ground more easily with runners under it than without them. Later, people discovered that wheels made movement even easier. But runners work better than wheels in sand and in marshes. Wheels sink into sand. They get stuck in swamps and marshes. Runners don't. Because of this, people in Lapland still use horse-drawn sledges to carry hay over marshy areas.

Who invented the wheel?

No one knows exactly who invented it or when. But we do know that people were using it about 5,000 years ago. These people lived in the areas now known as Iraq, Syria, and Turkey. The first wheels were probably round slices of a log.

The idea for the wheel probably came from log "rollers." People used to place logs under a large object. They would then roll the object across the logs. But there was a problem with this method. As soon as the object passed over a log, the log had to be carried to the front of the object again.

Without the wheel we would have no cars, trains, airplanes, watches, clocks, movie projectors, or washing machines!

What was the first vehicle with wheels?

The chariot may have been the first wheeled vehicle. It was a two-wheeled cart, open at the back. At first, a chariot was pulled by donkeys. Then horses replaced the donkeys. People who rode in chariots did not sit in them—they stood. Many ancient peoples—the Greeks and the Romans, for example—used them when fighting wars. Sometimes a soldier would stand in the chariot with the horse's reins tied to his waist. Then his hands were free to hold a spear and to fight.

Around the same time that the chariot was invented, other vehicles were developed. Four-wheeled wagons and many styles of two-wheeled carts were used for carrying loads.

Etruscan chariot

6

When did people start using carriages?

About 2,000 years ago ancient Romans were using carriages—horse-drawn vehicles for carrying seated people. But carriages were most popular in Europe and America in the 1700s. They remained popular through the 1800s. During that time carriages were lightweight, fast, and graceful.

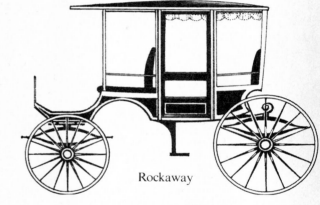

Rockaway

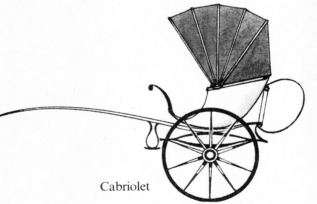

Cabriolet

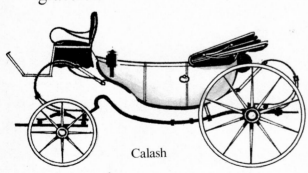

Calash

Buggy

What were some different kinds of carriages?

Here are pictures of a few kinds of carriages. They were all pulled by horses—from one to six, depending on the type of carriage.

7

How did it feel to ride in a cabriolet?

The cabriolet (cab-ree-uh-LAY) must have given a very gentle, bouncy ride. It was a lightweight carriage. But it had heavy-duty springs under the seat. When a trotting horse pulled the cabriolet over the unpaved roads of the 1800s, the carriage leaped in rhythm.

The French word "cabriolet" means little leap. It comes from an older French word for baby goat. Riding in a cabriolet probably reminded someone of riding on the back of a playful baby goat.

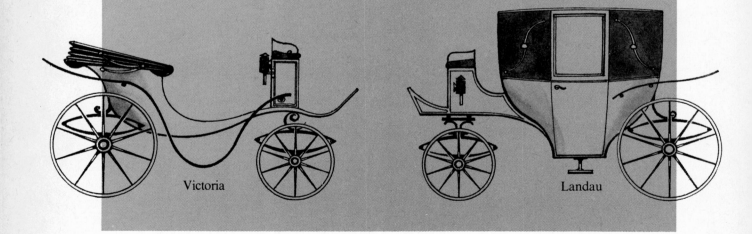

Which carriages did rich Europeans use?

The victoria and the landau were used by rich and royal Europeans. These carriages were made of fine woods and metals. From the outside the landau looked like a jewel box on wheels. Inside it often had velvet and satin seats and gold-trimmed walls.

Victoria

Landau

What was a coach?

Do you remember Cinderella? She rode in a coach when she went to the ball. A coach was a large, four-wheeled carriage. It was closed on the sides and on top. After the 1500s coaches were used in Europe for public transportation. Rich people owned their own private ones. However, their rides were no more comfortable than those of other people. Early roads were very bumpy. Springs were not put under carriage seats until the late 1700s. So, for the first 200 years, even a king had a rough ride!

What was a stagecoach?

A stagecoach was a coach that carried passengers, mail, and sometimes large packages. The inside of the coach seated from four to eight people. The mail, packages, and luggage were placed on the roof, on special racks.

Stagecoaches traveled on regular routes between two or more cities. The drivers changed horses at set stops, or "stages," along the routes. That's how stagecoaches got their name.

These vehicles became popular in Europe in the late 1600s and in America in the late 1700s. After 1825 stagecoaches were slowly replaced by railroads.

What sort of vehicles did American pioneers use to travel west?

American pioneers traveled west in covered wagons pulled by teams of horses. True to its name, a covered wagon was covered by a high, curved canvas top. Pioneer families took their household belongings with them in these sturdy wagons. Usually groups of families traveled together. Their wagons would follow a trail, one behind the other. The long line of wagons was called a wagon train.

Have people ever pulled carts?

Yes. Starting in 1870, men in Japan, China, and some other Asian countries pulled carts that were used as taxicabs. The carts were called rickshas, or jinrickishas (jin-RICK-shaws). A man stood at the front between two poles attached to the ricksha. He held the two poles and ran. In this way, he often pulled passengers 20 to 30 miles a day.

In most Asian countries rickshas have been outlawed. Pedicabs have replaced them. A pedicab is a three-wheeled cart. It has two wheels in the front with a passenger cart over them. The back looks like the back half of a bicycle. A driver sits on it and pedals.

Who invented the bicycle?

A Frenchman, Comte Mède de Sivrac (cawnt med duh see-VROCK), built an early wooden model in 1790. It had no pedals and no steering bar. A rider had to move and steer by putting his feet on the ground and pushing. De Sivrac's bicycle should have been called a "walking machine."

In about 1816 a German, Baron Karl von Drais, built a model with a steering bar. And in 1839 foot pedals were finally added by a Scottish blacksmith named Kirkpatrick Macmillan. This bicycle was much more like the ones we see today.

An early bicycle called a penny-farthing had a front wheel about nine times larger than the back wheel!

How does a bicycle work?

Between the two large wheels of a bicycle is a much smaller wheel with little teeth on it. This small wheel is called a sprocket. The foot pedals are attached to this sprocket. When a rider pushes the foot pedals, the sprocket turns. One end of a chain fits around the sprocket. The other end fits around a smaller sprocket in the center of the rear wheel of the bicycle. When the large sprocket turns, so does the chain. It turns the small sprocket and the large rear wheel. The bicycle moves forward.

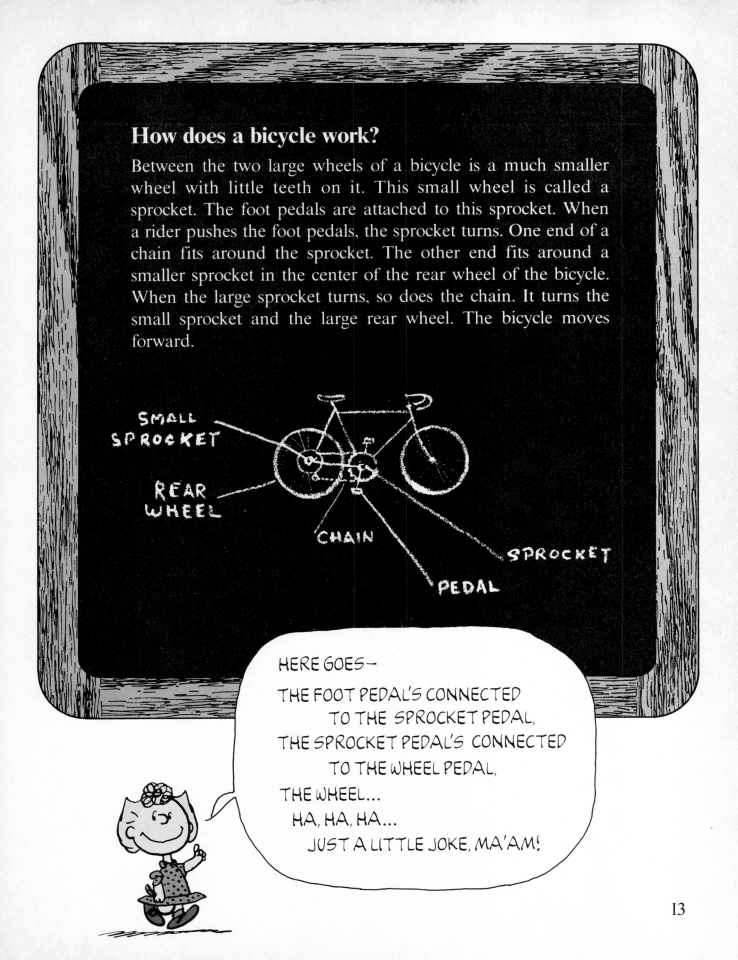

SMALL
SPROCKET

REAR
WHEEL

CHAIN

SPROCKET

PEDAL

HERE GOES—

THE FOOT PEDAL'S CONNECTED
TO THE SPROCKET PEDAL,
THE SPROCKET PEDAL'S CONNECTED
TO THE WHEEL PEDAL,
THE WHEEL...
HA, HA, HA...
JUST A LITTLE JOKE, MA'AM!

What was the longest bicycle ever built?

You've probably heard of a bicycle built for two. Well, the longest bicycle was built for 35! It was made in Denmark in 1976. The bike weighed more than a ton and was 72 feet (22 meters) long. That's longer than a dozen regular bicycles placed end to end.

What is the smallest bicycle ever built?

The world's smallest ridable bicycle has wheels just over 2 inches (5 centimeters) high. The bike weighs only two pounds (less than one kilogram). It is so small, it fits in the palm of its builder's hand. Yet he actually rides it at Circus Circus Hotel in Nevada.

How fast can you go on a bicycle?

The average bike rider can cycle up to 12 miles (19 kilometers) an hour. One cyclist reached 140½ miles (225 kilometers) an hour! But he did not go that fast by pedaling alone. He was riding his bicycle right behind a windscreen mounted on a car. The windscreen pushed the air out to the sides so that it did not slow down the movement of the bike and the rider.

Why do people put training wheels on children's bicycles?

If you have learned to ride a bicycle, you know how hard balancing it can be at first. A bicycle tips over when it's standing still. It tips over easily when moving slowly, too. A bike can balance itself only when it is moving very fast. Training wheels help children who haven't learned to pick up speed quickly. The training wheels keep the bike from tipping over until it is moving fast enough to balance itself.

LETS SEE...THAT JUST LEAVES 5 HOURS AND 24 MINUTES MORE TO GO.

One man balanced on a bike for 5 hours and 25 minutes—staying absolutely still!

How do training wheels balance a bicycle?

Training wheels make a bike very hard to tip over. Try this experiment to see why: Stand up straight with your feet close together. Ask someone—someone trustworthy!—to give you a gentle push sideways. With your feet close together, it is easy to fall over. You probably have to take a step to keep from falling. Now stand with your feet about as far apart as your shoulders. Ask your trustworthy person to give you another gentle push—just as hard as before. This time it is much easier to keep from falling over. With your feet farther apart, you are more stable because you have a wider base. The bicycle is the same. Without training wheels, it tips over easily. But when you attach training wheels to it, you make its base much wider. You would have to push the bicycle quite hard to make it fall onto its side.

Why do small children ride on tricycles?

Just as a bicycle with training wheels is hard to tip over, so is a three-wheeled tricycle. When small children ride tricycles, they don't have to worry about balance. They can just have fun!

15

What is a motorcycle?

A motorcycle is any two-wheeled vehicle powered by a gasoline engine. There are several different kinds. Each kind except for the heaviest has a special name. The heaviest motorcycles are called simply motorcycles. They have no engine cover. You can see the engine between the two wheels.

What's the difference between a motorbike and a motor scooter?

They are both kinds of motorcycles, but they are built differently.

A motorbike is very lightweight. It looks a lot like a bicycle with an engine.

A motor scooter looks more like an electric cart than like a bicycle or an ordinary motorcycle. It is wider and heavier than a motorbike but lighter than a standard motorcycle. Its body is covered by a frame which hides the engine.

What was a horseless carriage?

"Horseless carriage" was the nickname given to the first automobiles. And that's exactly what they were—carriages that moved without being pulled by horses. Instead of horses pulling them, automobiles had their own engines. They practically moved themselves. In fact the word "automobile" means self-moving.

How did a steam-powered automobile work?

It had a steam engine that boiled water and turned it to steam. Inside the engine was a piece of metal called a piston. The steam pushed the piston back and forth. The piston turned a metal rod that was connected to the car's wheels. When the rod moved, the wheels moved—and so did the car.

WHAT THOSE HORSES NEEDED WAS A GOOD STRONG UNION!

Why didn't steam-driven cars last?

Steam-driven cars were unpopular for several reasons. They were so noisy they frightened both horses and people. These cars dirtied the air with smoke wherever they went. And sometimes even hot coals would shoot out of them.

But that was not all. Stagecoach and railroad line owners did not like the new automobiles. They were afraid that if many people rode in these cars, fewer passengers would ride on their lines. In England stagecoach and railroad owners were able to have laws passed that limited the use of steam-driven cars. For example, one law of 1865 said that a signal man had to walk in front of each car and warn people it was coming!

1910 Stanley Steamer

What is an electric car?

An electric car is an automobile powered by one or more electric motors. This means that the motor gets its power from a battery. The battery must be plugged into a wall socket from time to time to be recharged.

Electric cars were popular in the 1890s and early 1900s. They were clean and quiet. They could move as fast as 20 miles (32 kilometers) an hour. But after an electric car had traveled only about 50 miles (80 kilometers), the battery went dead. Because the battery had to be recharged often, people quickly tired of the electric car. Inventors worked to develop a new kind of engine. And they did—the gasoline engine. Gasoline engines were more powerful than electric ones. They cost less to run and their batteries lasted longer.

Who are the "fathers of the modern automobile"?

Two Germans, Gottlieb Daimler and Karl Benz, are considered the fathers of the modern automobile. In 1885, each man, working separately, developed a new kind of engine. It was the kind of gasoline engine we use in cars today. Daimler put his engine in a motorcycle. Benz put his engine in a three-wheeled automobile.

Benz's three-wheel car

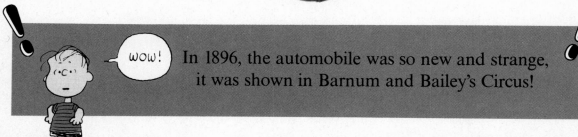

WOW! In 1896, the automobile was so new and strange, it was shown in Barnum and Bailey's Circus!

18

How does the engine of a modern car work?

When the engine is turned on, gasoline goes to a part of the engine called the carburetor (CAR-buh-ray-tur). There, the gasoline mixes with air. The gas and air mixture goes to the cylinders (SILL-in-durz). A car usually has four, six, or eight cylinders. A cylinder is a hollow container that is shaped much like a tin can. In each cylinder is a piston, a solid piece of metal that moves up and down. A piston moves down to suck in the gasoline and air mixture. When it moves up again, it causes a spark plug to give off an electric spark. This in turn causes the mixture to explode. The heat of the explosion pushes the piston down again. This happens in one cylinder after another, providing the energy to move the car.

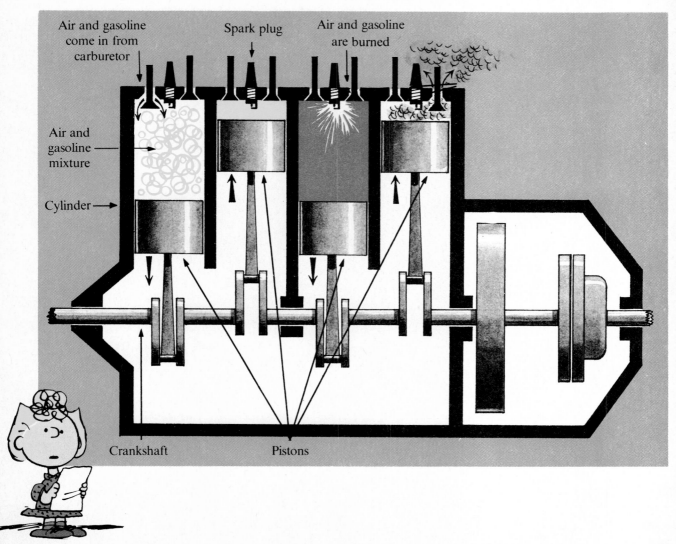

Who was Henry Ford?

Henry Ford was an American pioneer in building cars. He introduced the moving assembly line. Each worker on an assembly line does just one small job in putting a car together. The parts are on a moving belt. When a worker finishes his or her job, the parts move along to the next worker. Before using Ford's method, workers spent a lot of time doing complicated jobs to make each car. Because of the moving assembly line, factories were able to produce cars more quickly and cheaply than before. Ford could sell his cars for less than other cars, so more people could afford to own them.

Henry Ford

By the 1920's a finished Model T Ford came off the assembly line every 10 seconds!

What was the Model T?

The Model T was Ford's most famous car. The Ford Motor Company built it between 1908 and 1927. To keep the price down, Ford made only small changes in the Model T each year.

THAT'S VERY INTERESTING

One 1936 Ford has been driven more than 1 million 37 thousand miles (1 million 659 thousand kilometers)!

Where does gasoline come from?

Gasoline is made from petroleum. Petroleum is a thick, oily liquid found deep inside the earth. People drill thousands of feet into the ground to get to it. Americans usually call petroleum "oil."

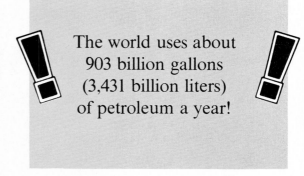

The world uses about 903 billion gallons (3,431 billion liters) of petroleum a year!

What are the dials and knobs on a car's dashboard?

The knobs control the lights, the heater, the windshield wipers, the air conditioner, and the radio. The dials tell a driver how much gas and oil are in the car. They also show how fast the driver is going and if the battery is making or losing electricity.

Why do we put motor oil in our cars?

A car's engine has moving parts. We use motor oil (which is made from petroleum) to keep the engine's parts moving smoothly. The oil provides a thin layer of greasy liquid on the parts. Then they don't get rusty, scrape against each other, or wear out quickly.

21

Why do cars have license plates?

All states make car owners register their cars. License plates are part of this registration. A license plate can help the police find a stolen car. It can also help identify a car in case of an accident. Finally, states use car registration as a way to check the safety of automobiles. Some states force car owners to have their cars checked once or twice a year. Unless the car meets the state's safety standards, the owner cannot renew the car's registration.

 Every year about 7 million cars end up in junkyards!

22

Why do you need seat belts and shoulder harnesses in a car?

Seat belts and shoulder harnesses keep passengers from being thrown into the windshield, onto the floor, or out of the car during an accident. So seat belts and shoulder harnesses help prevent serious injuries and save lives.

SECURITY IS WHEN THE SEAT BELT CAN STRETCH AROUND YOU AND YOUR BLANKET.

MY MOM AND DAD WERE GOING ON A LITTLE VACATION, BUT THEY CHANGED THEIR MINDS

MOM IS KIND OF A WORRIER

SHE SAYS, WHAT IF THEY WERE DRIVING ALONG THE FREEWAY DOING ABOUT SEVENTY, AND SUDDENLY SOMETHING WENT WRONG WITH THE GLOVE COMPARTMENT?

THAT IS SOMETHING TO WORRY ABOUT

What does a speed limit on a road mean?

Usually a speed limit tells a driver the fastest speed at which it is safe to drive on a certain road. (Occasionally it also tells the slowest speed.) Some roads post only one speed limit. Other roads post different speed limits depending on the weather.

The United States has a national highway speed limit of 55 miles (88 kilometers) an hour. This limit is meant to save gasoline as well as lives. When moving at higher speeds, automobiles waste gasoline.

If a car goes over the speed limit, the driver may be stopped by a policeman and given a speeding ticket. The driver then has to pay a fine. If he gets too many speeding tickets, the state government will take away his driver's license.

TELL YOUR DAD I'LL WASH HIS CAR FOR A DOLLAR

HE WANTS TO KNOW IF YOU HAVE WORKMAN'S COMPENSATION.. WHAT HAPPENS IF YOU'RE INJURED ON THE JOB?

TELL HIM I ONLY WASH CARS THAT ARE STANDING STILL!

There are more automobiles in the state of California than in all of Europe!

23

Why do some racing cars look so strange?

Racing cars are built for speed and power. Many cars, like those in the Grand Prix (grawn pree) races, have sleek bodies. They are built narrow and close to the ground. Most racing cars also have very wide tires. These tires are good for going around corners very fast. They also help give the car power. Some racing cars even have "wings" mounted on their backs. These wings, also called aerofoil (AIR-o-foyl) tails, are not meant to lift the cars off the ground. In fact, they do just the opposite. They help the cars stay down on the road, which makes them go faster.

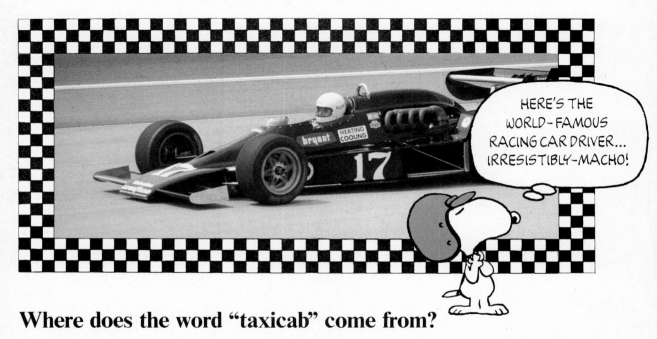

HERE'S THE WORLD-FAMOUS RACING CAR DRIVER... IRRESISTIBLY-MACHO!

Where does the word "taxicab" come from?

Although people were hiring carriages and other vehicles for thousands of years, the name "taxicab" wasn't used until the 1800s. The "cab" in "taxicab" is short for "cabriolet" (cab-ree-uh-LAY), a type of one-horse carriage. People hired cabriolets to carry them over short distances. Inside the cabriolet was a taximeter (TACK-see-mee-tur), a machine which kept track of the fare due for the ride. Modern taxicabs have taximeters in them, too. "Taxi" is short for "taximeter."

In October 1929, New York City had 29,000 taxis. That is the largest fleet of taxis that has ever existed in one city!

What kind of car have astronauts used on the moon?

On each of three Apollo moon expeditions, astronauts traveled on the moon's surface in a lunar rover. A rover looks something like a jeep or a dune buggy. But its top and sides are completely open. There is no need to cover the astronaut riders since the moon has no wind and no rain. However, the rover does have fenders. Its moving wheels stir up dust. The fenders keep the dust from blowing in the astronauts' faces. A lunar rover runs on battery power. It has no engine.

What happened to the lunar rovers? All three were left on the moon!

Lunar roving vehicle

Why do we have public transportation?

Years ago most people lived close enough to their jobs to walk to them. But as cities grew, people often had to work farther away from home. They needed a way to get around. Owning a carriage cost too much. So bus and streetcar lines were built. They carried many people at one time and charged only a small fare. More recently, subways and commuter trains have carried many riders, too.

Some people drive their cars to work. But good public transportation is much better than cars in a city. Too many cars dirty the air and cause traffic jams. Buses, trains, and streetcars take up less room than the cars needed to carry the same number of people. They also cause less pollution. City parking is hard to find and expensive for cars. But there are no parking problems for people who take public transportation.

25

Where does the word "bus" come from?

The word "bus" is short for "omnibus," which means for everyone.

What were early buses like?

The first buses were simply large carriages drawn by horses. One of the earliest buses carried people around Paris as long ago as 1662. New York City started bus service in 1829 with its "sociable." The sociable was a carriage with enough room to seat ten people. In the same year, London produced its first omnibus. The omnibus was pulled by three horses side by side. This caused terrible traffic jams. The streets weren't wide enough for the omnibus and other traffic, too. Later omnibuses were made narrower and could be pulled by two horses.

Why was the double-decker bus invented?

The London omnibus was very popular. So many people wanted to ride it that there wasn't room for everyone. Some people used to hold on to the roof. Because of this, a long bus seat was added to the roof of the carriage in 1847. Seats on the open top were half-price. Later, a canopy was added to protect passengers from rain and sun. Today double-decker buses run in cities such as London and New York. But the new ones have closed tops.

What are the longest buses in the world?

The longest buses are each 76 feet (23 meters) long. That's twice as long as an average bus. These very long buses have room enough to seat 121 people. They are used in the Middle East.

San Francisco cable car

What is a streetcar?

A streetcar is any vehicle that moves along rails which are set into the surface of the road. It usually runs within city limits. Early streetcars were pulled by horses. The horses didn't have to work as hard pulling streetcars as they did pulling buses. The rails made their task easier. At the same time, the passengers got a smoother ride.

There are two kinds of streetcars. They get their power, not from horses, but from electricity. One modern streetcar is the trolley car. It gets its power from an overhead electric line. The other modern streetcar is the cable car. It is pulled by a heavy steel rope called a cable. The cable moves along a slot under the surface of the street.

New York State ski gondola

How are cable cars used?

Cable cars are used to climb steep hills and mountains. In San Francisco, the hills are so steep that buses and trolleys have trouble climbing them. So cable cars do the job.

There is a second kind of cable car that is not a streetcar. This kind hangs from steel ropes that are strung between tall towers. As the cables move, the car moves. Such cable cars are often used to take passengers up mountains. You can see these cable cars in many ski areas.

Hanging cable cars carry more than passengers. They also carry things such as tools and supplies.

Why do streetcars and trains run on rails?

A vehicle running on rails doesn't hit holes, ruts, mud, or bumps as a car or a wagon on the road does. Also, pulling a car on rails takes less energy, or effort, than pulling a car of the same weight along a road. When a car runs on rails there is less friction, or rubbing, to hold back the wheels. So they roll faster and more freely.

When did people first start using trains?

The very first trains were used by miners before 1600. These trains had no motors and they weren't pulled by animals. They were simple wooden tubs which the miners pushed along wooden rails. Later, miners used horses for pulling wagons along the tracks.

An early train used a "horse engine." The horse ran on an endless belt which was connected to the train's wheels!

Another early train used a sail. The wind moved the train along the rails!

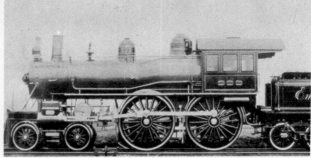

When was the first railroad built?

The first public railroad was built in England in 1825. It ran along 20 miles (32 kilometers) of metal tracks. At first the plan was to have horses pull the trains. But the railroad company decided to use steam engines instead. Each steam engine was able to pull a much heavier load than horses would have been able to pull. Because of this, the railroad was a great success. Five years later an even bigger railroad was built in England.

How fast were the first railroad trains?

In 1830 a steam locomotive named "Rocket" reached a speed of 29 miles (46 kilometers) an hour. People thought that was very fast. And it *was* for that time—for the average train moved at about 15 miles (24 kilometers) an hour.

! Laid end to end, the tracks of the world's main railroad routes would stretch 750,000 miles (1,200,000 kilometers). That's almost three times the distance between the earth and the moon! **!**

How fast are modern trains?

The average modern train travels at about 65 miles (104 kilometers) an hour. However, some trains today average more than 100 miles (160 kilometers) an hour.

What is a locomotive?

A locomotive is the railroad car that holds the train's engine. Most locomotives are at the front of a train and pull it. But some are at the back of a train and push it, instead. People sometimes use the word "locomotive" to mean the engine itself.

How do modern trains run?

Most modern trains are pulled by locomotives that use diesel-electric engines. A diesel-electric engine is similar to a gasoline engine. But it burns oil instead of gasoline. The oil-burning diesel turns generators. These generators supply electrical energy to turn the locomotive's wheels.

Some locomotives are fully electric. They use no oil. They get electric current from wires hung above the railroad track or from a third rail that runs on the ground inside the track. As in the diesel engine, the electric power turns the train wheels.

Do American railroads make most of their money from passengers?

No. In the United States about $95.00 out of every $100.00 that railroads earn comes from carrying freight. Freight includes packages, metals, animals, and lumber. In the United States as many as ten thousand freight trains are on the move every day. In Europe, however, passenger trains are quite popular.

What's the longest freight train on record?

The longest freight train stretched 4 miles (more than 6 kilometers). It was made up of 500 coal cars and 6 diesel locomotives—3 at the front and 3 at about the middle of the train. This freight train traveled 157 miles (251 kilometers) on the Norfolk and Western Railway on November 15, 1967. The train weighed 47,000 tons (42,300 metric tons). An average freight train has about 100 cars.

Why are freight trains so long?

One reason is that many railroads are being asked to carry more freight than ever before. A second reason is that different kinds of freight cars are needed to carry different kinds of freight.

For example, boxcars carry grains, cans, and packages. Boxcars are completely enclosed. Flatcars are open platforms used for carrying logs, steel, machinery, and even automobiles. Stock cars carry cattle, pigs, or sheep. And tank cars hold liquids, such as oil. There are also refrigerator cars, poultry cars, and milk cars—to name a few.

The Trans-Siberian Railroad in the U.S.S.R.
is so long that it would stretch from New York
to California and back again!

John Massis moved two cars of a train
by pulling them with his teeth.
The cars weighed 80 tons
(72 metric tons)!

ANYWAY...
MOST OF THE CREDIT SHOULD
GO TO HIS MOTHER WHO
PROBABLY MADE HIM BRUSH
AFTER EVERY MEAL
—RIGHT SIR?...

Why are railroad tunnels built?

Most railroad tunnels are built through the rock of hills and mountains. Instead of winding miles and miles of tracks around a mountain, builders prefer to cut through the mountain in a straight line. Then the train route is shorter—and safer, too!

How is a railroad tunnel built?

Workers drill holes deep into the side of a hill or a mountain. They pack explosives such as dynamite into the holes. Huge sections of rock and earth are blasted away in seconds. The workers clear away the loose rock and drill more holes. After they have cleared the tunnel all the way through, they line it with concrete. Then they lay down tracks. Now the railroad tunnel is ready to be used.

What do train whistles mean?

Locomotive engineers use train whistles to signal to crew members and other railroad workers. Whistles also warn people and animals that a train is coming. "Whistle talk" is a code made up of short and long toots. For example, one short toot means "Apply brakes. Stop." Two long toots are a signal to release the train's brakes and start moving.

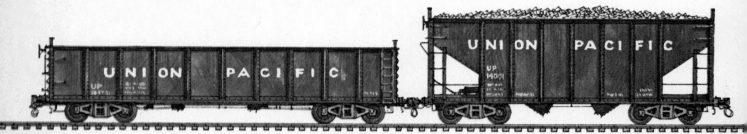

How do railroads prevent accidents?

Railroads have many ways of preventing accidents besides train-whistle warnings. One of these is the block signal system. A block is a length of railroad track, usually one or two miles long. To prevent collisions, only one train at a time is allowed in a block. Colored lights signal whether a train may enter a block. Red means stop. Green means go. And yellow means go ahead with caution. When one train is already in a block, the signals warn other trains to stop. Some block signals are hand-operated. Railroad people along the line control those signals. Other block signals work automatically.

Some locomotives have special panels on which signals give the same information as the signal lights on the tracks. If an engineer does not notice a panel signal to stop, the train will stop automatically. Finally, crew members use two-way radios to speak with faraway stations and train yards.

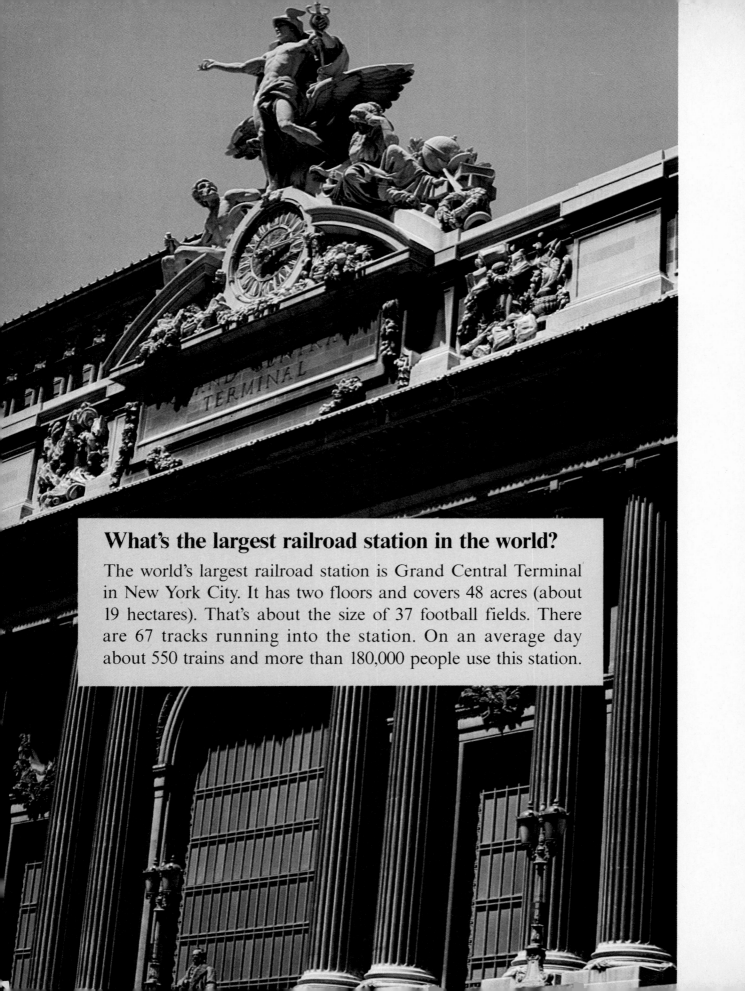

What's the largest railroad station in the world?

The world's largest railroad station is Grand Central Terminal in New York City. It has two floors and covers 48 acres (about 19 hectares). That's about the size of 37 football fields. There are 67 tracks running into the station. On an average day about 550 trains and more than 180,000 people use this station.

What is a monorail?

A monorail is a railroad that has only one rail. Most railroads have two. This rail may be above or below the monorail cars. Monorail cars are often powered by gasoline engines or electric motors. Monorails are faster and cheaper to run than two-rail lines.

What is a subway?

A subway is a passenger railroad that runs mostly underground. It gets its power from electricity. Because it is underground, a subway is perfect for a crowded city. Except for its station entrances, it does not take up any street space. Since subways carry people all around a city, they must make many stops along their routes.

When was the first city subway opened?

The first subway was opened in London, England, on January 10, 1863. The trains used steam locomotives that burned coke (later coal). It was nicknamed "the sewer," for it smelled horrible, and was terribly dirty and dark. Some passengers carried candles to light their way. Pickpockets were always at work. Nonetheless, this first subway carried nearly 10 million passengers in its first year.

Which is the busiest subway system in the world?

The busiest subway system in the world belongs to New York City. In 1970, New York's subways carried more than 2 billion passengers. By 1976, the number had gone down to about 1 billion 27 million. But so far, New York's subways are still the busiest.

How many cities in the world have subways?

There are 67 subways in the world today. Besides New York, some of the cities with large subway systems are Paris, London, Berlin, Moscow, Hamburg, Tokyo, and Boston. Not all cities call them "subways," however. Some have the name "metro" and others "underground."

The Tokyo, Japan, subway system hires special workers to squeeze passengers into crowded trains!

What will trains of the future be like?

Some future trains will have no wheels! Instead they may be lifted above the tracks by an air cushion or by magnets. Such trains would be very quiet. And they would not wear out quickly because they would not rub against the tracks. Magnetic trains are already being tested.

Trains of an even more distant future may run by gravity—the force which pulls everything on earth toward its center. The trains would move through a long airless tunnel. Both ends of the tunnel would slant steeply toward the center. The train would run downhill to the middle of the tunnel. By then it would be moving at a speed of many thousands of miles an hour. This is so fast that the train would be able to travel to the other end of the tunnel before slowing to a stop.

Twin tank truck

Why are there many different kinds of trucks?

Many different kinds of trucks are needed to do many different kinds of jobs. Refrigerator trucks carry food that would spoil if it were not kept cold. Tank trucks carry liquids such as gasoline. Dump trucks tilt so they can unload things easily. Tractors and trailers carry huge loads over long distances. Small enclosed trucks called panel trucks carry small loads over short distances. Vans are long trucks that move furniture. And bottle trucks have special racks for holding cases of bottles.

These are only a few examples of the many kinds of trucks. More than 600 companies in the United States build thousands of special kinds of trucks. Today there are more than 12 million trucks in the United States.

Flat-bed trailer

Motor vehicle transporter

What is a trailer?

A trailer is a van or wagon that is pulled by another vehicle. It has no engine of its own. One kind of trailer, called a mobile home, can be pulled by a car or a truck. It is outfitted with beds, seats, and even a bathroom and a kitchen. Many people spend their vacations traveling around in trailers. Other people live in them all the time.

Another kind of trailer carries freight. It is so big that it must be pulled by a powerful tractor truck.

40

Three-wheel truck

What is a tractor truck?

A tractor truck is the front part of a big tractor-trailer, or "rig." It contains the engine and the cab, where the driver sits. The tractor truck can be driven without the trailer, but the trailer can't be driven without the tractor. The trailer has no engine of its own. Power for the trailer's brakes and lights comes from the tractor truck.

Dump truck

Cement truck

KEEP ON TRUCKIN'!!

HA HA

HA HA HA

41

What were the first fire trucks like?

The first fire trucks were simply water pumps on wheels that men pulled to fires. Europeans used those simple hand trucks in the 1500s.

In the early 1800s, American fire companies used steam pumps, or engines, pulled by men or horses. Fire companies tried to outdo each other by hiring artists to paint beautiful scenes on the sides of their engines. They gave the engines fancy names such as "Live Oak" and "Ocean Wave."

Fire horses of the early 1900s were well trained.
As soon as the fire alarm rang, the horses trotted out
from their stalls by themselves and
stood ready in front of the fire trucks!

What were the first ambulances like?

The first ambulances were probably horse-drawn carts. The Spanish army used them to carry its wounded off the battlefield in 1487. Before that armies probably used litters and stretchers to carry wounded soldiers.

How do people travel across snow?

Wheels sink into snow. So people have invented ways of gliding over it. People have made snowshoes and skis. They have also made vehicles with runners such as sleds, sleighs, and snowmobiles.

What are snowshoes?

Snowshoes are made of light, wooden frames that have strings of leather stretched across them. They look something like long oval tennis rackets. They have straps that fasten to a person's boots. Someone wearing snowshoes can walk on deep snow without sinking into it. Snowshoes work because they spread a person's weight over a large area.

American Indians invented snowshoes. Today people wear them while hunting, farming, taking care of forests, or just for fun. People who wear snowshoes usually use ski poles or special ice picks to help them keep their balance.

When did people start using skis?

People have used skis for more than 5,000 years. Skiing began as a way of getting around in places where there was a lot of snow. The first skis were probably made from animal bones.

What is cross-country skiing?

When you go cross-country skiing, you don't just go down hills. You may ski uphill, downhill, or on flat land. Cross-country skiers usually ski long distances, often on country trails. Their skis are narrower and lighter than downhill skis.

What are sleds and sleighs?

A sled is a vehicle on runners. People use sleds for much more than playing in the snow. Until snowmobiles were invented, sleds pulled by dogs were the only vehicles that could move people and things over the ice and the snow.

A sleigh is a kind of sled with curved runners. Its seat is a foot or more above the ground. Horse-drawn sleighs were very popular before people had automobiles with snow tires.

What are snowmobiles?

Snowmobiles are sleds with motors. Instead of long runners, snowmobiles have two short skis in front. The rider steers the skis with handlebars. At the back is a wide belt made for gripping the snow.

Most snowmobiles can speed along at 50 miles (80 kilometers) an hour. Some can go faster than 100 miles (160 kilometers) an hour. In some snowy places, snowmobiles are the only fast way to get around. So they are important to ski patrols, doctors, and the police. Today, Eskimos usually use snowmobiles instead of dog sleds. And many people ride them and race them just for fun.

Snowmobile race

What is a toboggan?

A toboggan is a vehicle without runners that glides on snow and ice. A toboggan is made of long strips of wood that curl up at the front. The underside of a toboggan is highly polished. So it glides easily and moves very fast.

American Indians made the first toboggans to carry things across snow. Today, people still use toboggans to carry things. But they are more popular as vehicles for sport. People coast down hills in toboggans or down special long, straight trails.

Charlie Brown on the Sea

How did people first cross rivers and streams?

If the water was too deep to walk through, they probably swam. But only the strongest swimmers could have gotten across a wide river. Some early, tired swimmer probably grabbed onto a floating log. He or she became the first person to use a raft—a simple platform that floats on water.

What were early rafts like?

One log, and then two logs tied together, were probably the first rafts. A rider had nothing to paddle with but his hands. Later a person most likely used a stick to push the raft through the water. Still later people discovered that a flat piece of wood worked better than a stick. It made the raft go faster. And so the paddle was invented.

In some parts of the world people built other kinds of rafts. In Egypt, for example, they tied together bundles of sticks or heavy reeds.

"Kon-Tiki"

What is the "Kon-Tiki"?

The "Kon-Tiki" is one of the most famous rafts in the world. It was built in 1947 by Thor Heyerdahl (HI-ur-doll), a Norwegian scientist. The "Kon-Tiki" is a copy of the rafts used by natives of the South Pacific. It is made of balsa, a light wood that floats easily. Heyerdahl sailed the tiny "Kon-Tiki" thousands of miles across the Pacific Ocean. He went from South America to Polynesia (pol-uh-NEE-zhuh)—a group of islands south of Hawaii. Heyerdahl's voyage proves that people could have made the same trip by raft 1,500 years ago. So it is possible that the people of Polynesia are the great, great, great . . . grandchildren of South American Indians.

Reed boats in Lake Titicaca

What were the first boats like?

The first boats developed from rafts. To keep dry, people turned up the sides of their reed rafts. In this way, they invented a saucer-shaped boat. Then people made longer, narrower boats. Long boats are easier to steer than round ones. The narrower shape allows boats to move through the water faster.

What is a canoe?

A canoe is a long, narrow boat that is pointed at both ends. One, two, or three people sit in the canoe, facing the front, or bow (rhymes with cow). They use a paddle, or paddles, to move the canoe through the water and steer it. Canoes were among the first kinds of small boats.

What did the earliest Americans use when they traveled by water?

The earliest Americans, Indians, used canoes. They had two kinds—dugout and birchbark. Which kind of canoe they used depended on where they lived. In the north, where birch trees grew, Indians made birchbark canoes. In other places they made dugouts.

How did the Indians make a dugout canoe?

A dugout canoe was made from a long, thick log. The canoe-maker burned the middle of the log partway through. Then he scraped or dug out the inside to make it hollow.

Dugout canoes are very heavy, and move slowly through the water. But they are very strong.

What is a birchbark canoe like?

A birchbark canoe is made of bark strips peeled from birch trees. The person making the canoe sews the strips together, using tree roots for thread. He then attaches the bark to a wooden frame.

Birchbark canoes are much lighter than dugout canoes. They can be carried easily from one stream to another. Dugout canoes are too heavy to be carried very far.

 In 1928, a man crossed the Atlantic Ocean in a canoe with a sail. The trip took 58 days!

Are canoes still used today?

Yes, people still use canoes. In certain places, such as Africa and the South Pacific islands, people still travel by canoe. But in most other parts of the world, canoes are used mainly for fun. People take them on hunting or fishing trips or on camping holidays. Today, most canoes are made by machine, not by hand. And they are not all made of wood. Now some canoes are made of canvas, light metal, or plastic.

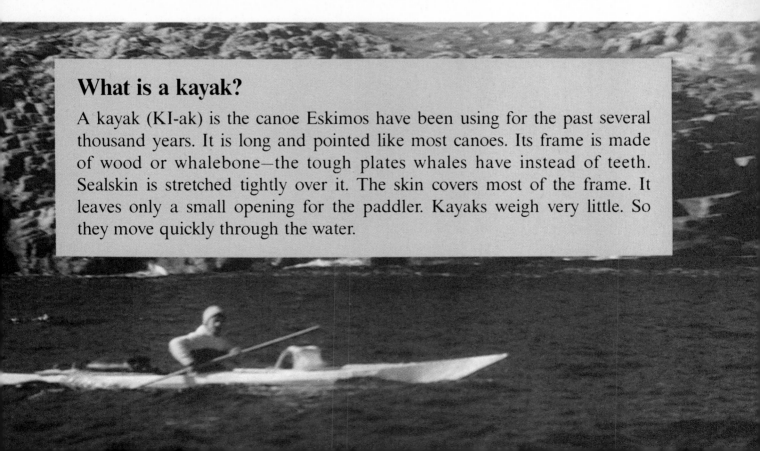

What is a kayak?

A kayak (KI-ak) is the canoe Eskimos have been using for the past several thousand years. It is long and pointed like most canoes. Its frame is made of wood or whalebone—the tough plates whales have instead of teeth. Sealskin is stretched tightly over it. The skin covers most of the frame. It leaves only a small opening for the paddler. Kayaks weigh very little. So they move quickly through the water.

What is a rowboat?

A rowboat is any kind of boat that is moved by oars. An oar is longer than a paddle, but it's used in the same way. A simple rowboat seats one person. The rower usually uses two oars, one on each side of the boat. Many rowboats have oarlocks to hold the oars in place.

WHY DO YOU HAVE TO MAKE A BIG DEAL OUT OF EVERYTHING... I JUST SAID I'D TAKE YOU ROWING.

Why did people add sails to their boats?

A sail on a boat can catch the wind. This, in turn, causes the boat to move. The ancient Egyptians discovered this fact about 5,000 years ago. The first sails were made of thick materials that could trap the wind. Either a large square piece of linen or papyrus (puh-PIE-russ)—a heavy, coarse paper—was used.

The early sailors could travel only *with* the wind. If the wind was blowing in the wrong direction, they had to put down their sails and row the boat themselves. It was not until the triangular sail was invented that sailing in almost any direction became possible. This happened about 1,600 years ago.

Who were the first sailors to use ships?

The first people to use ships lived around the Mediterranean (med-ih-tuh-RAY-nee-un) Sea. Many of these people were from Egypt and Phoenicia (fih-NISH-uh), a land where Syria, Lebanon, and Israel are today.

The Egyptians started to do a great deal of sailing more than 4,000 years ago. They made easy-to-sail ships from wooden boards. They sailed these ships around the Mediterranean, trading with other countries. Then, about 3,000 years ago, the Phoenicians began to design ships both for trading and for fighting sea battles. They made long, fast ships for fighting. They made short, wide ones for trading.

Model of Egyptian galley ship rowed by slaves

Were ships ever built that used 50 oars?

One of the earliest ships, known as a galley, sometimes had 50 or more oars. Galleys were first used by the people who lived around the Mediterranean Sea more than 3,000 years ago. Galleys were rowed by slaves who sat on benches. Each man held an oar with both hands. And all the slaves rowed at the same time. The earliest galleys had no sails. But later ones did. Even so, their most important source of power was muscle. Most galleys also had one large oar at the back of the boat. It was used for steering.

Early Romans believed
that ships needed eyes to see.
So they painted eyes on their galleys!

What's the difference between boats and ships?

Boats are smaller than ships. And they rarely travel far out on the ocean. Ships do. They are large, seagoing vessels. Ships are used for trading, carrying passengers, and fighting battles.

Who thought of using more than one sail?

About 2,500 years ago, both the Greeks and the Phoenicians came up with a new idea in ship design. Until then, ships had always had one mast (pole for a sail) and one sail. The Greeks and the Phoenicians added a second mast and two more sails. The added sails gave them extra speed and better control of direction. About 2,000 years later, the Greeks added a third mast and a fourth sail.

Who were the Vikings?

The Vikings were fierce seagoing pirates from Norway, Denmark, and Sweden. They traveled by sea to raid other parts of Europe about 1,000 years ago. They probably traveled as far as America before the time of Columbus! The Vikings made some permanent settlements in England, Russia, Iceland, and Greenland.

The Vikings founded the city of Dublin, Ireland!

56

What kind of ships did the Vikings use?

Viking warships were long, narrow, and fast. They were usually open on top and had flat oak bottoms. They had many oars and just one sail. The earliest of these were called long ships. However, the later Viking ships were longer than the long ships. Each of these later ships had a wood carving at the front. The carving was of a person's head or of a monster, such as a dragon. The Vikings called these warships "drakkars"—dragons.

The Vikings had other kinds of ships, too. A wider ship, called a knorr (pronounce the "k"), carried goods for trading. Knorrs had fewer oars, so there was more room for cargo.

Why did people put "figureheads" on their ships?

Some figureheads served the same purpose as a name painted on a ship. They were used to identify the ship. Figureheads were also used to scare away evil spirits. Dragon heads and other monsters were common on Viking ships for that reason.

HEY, SISTER, I THINK YOU MISSED YOUR CALLING...YOU WOULD HAVE MADE A GREAT FIGUREHEAD!

57

Why is the right side of a ship called "starboard" and the left called "port"?

The Vikings were the first to use those names. A typical Viking ship had a giant steering oar. It was on the right side, near the back of the ship. It was there for two reasons. First, most people are right-handed. Second, the ancient people believed that the right side of a ship was stronger than the left side. The right side of a Viking ship was eventually called the "steerboard." We've changed it a little, to "starboard."

Because the steering oar was in the way, the Vikings could not dock on the right side of the ship. They always docked with the left side facing port. So that's what they called it—and so do we.

Why did Columbus sail west to get to the East?

Christopher Columbus believed that the world was round. Before his time (the late 1400s), just about everyone had assumed the world was flat. If the world really was round, Columbus thought, he should be able to reach the Indies—east of Europe—by sailing west. (The "Indies" was a name for India, China, and the islands of Southeast Asia.) In fact, Columbus believed the shortest route would be directly west across the Atlantic Ocean.

When Columbus reached America for the first time, he thought he was in the Indies. That's why he named the people there Indians!

58

What kind of ships did Christopher Columbus use for his famous 1492 voyage?

Two of Columbus's ships, the "Niña" and the "Pinta," were caravels. These light, fast sailing ships first became popular around 1400. They had three masts: the foremast (in the front), the mainmast (in the middle), and the mizzenmast (in the back). The foremast had a square sail. But the other two masts had sails in the shape of triangles.

The third ship—and the largest—was a carrack. Known as the "Santa María," it was the one Columbus himself traveled on. The ship had the same three masts as the caravels. But both the mainmast and the foremast had square sails. Only the mizzenmast had a sail in the shape of a triangle. A pole called a bowsprit stuck out from the front, or bow, of the ship. It held a small square sail.

Mainmast —

Mizzenmast —

Foremast —

— Bowsprit

The "Santa María"

Where did Columbus's crew sleep?

On the floor! Only the most important officers of the "Niña," the "Pinta," and the "Santa María" slept in bunks. The other men had to sleep on deck. However, after Columbus's first voyage to America, the men slept below deck in hammocks. The hammock was an American Indian invention which Columbus and his men adopted.

What is a galleon?

A galleon is a large wooden sailing ship which was popular in Europe during the mid-1500s. It was used for trading and, in wartime, for battle. A galleon was better for long-distance sea voyages than earlier sailing ships. It was much deeper. So it had bunk space for the whole crew.

The foremast and the mainmast of a galleon each have two or three sails. Sometimes the mizzenmast has two sails, also. Some of the early galleons had oars as well as sails. But galleons could be rowed only in smooth waters.

Was Magellan the first person to sail around the world?

Ferdinand Magellan always gets the credit. However, he never actually completed the trip around the world. But one of his ships did.

Magellan was a Spanish-Portuguese sailor. In 1519, he decided to try to find a short route to the Indies. He planned to go around the tip of South America and then west to Asia.

He left Spain with five ships. In two years Magellan got halfway around the world. During the voyage he was killed on a Pacific island. Of his five ships only one completed the trip. One ship was wrecked on a rock. One returned to Spain early when its crew mutinied (rebelled against Magellan). One was left, leaking badly, on a Pacific island. And one was lost on the way home.

What was the Spanish Armada?

For many years, no country was as mighty as Spain when it came to ocean travel. During the 1500s, Spain had the largest fleet of ships in Europe. It was known as the Spanish Armada. These ships were used by Spanish explorers to sail across the Atlantic Ocean to America. The Spaniards brought back many treasures from the New World. Spain became a very rich country.

The Armada also protected Spain from enemies and fought her battles when it was necessary. Because of its Armada, Spain was, for many years, one of the most powerful countries in Europe. But in 1588, a fleet of English ships defeated the Spanish Armada. The English then were masters of the sea.

The mighty Spanish Armada included 130 ships of war, 8,000 sailors, and 20,000 soldiers. The U.S. Navy today has 500 ships of war, 125 submarines, and 547,000 people!

What kind of ship was the "Mayflower"?

The ship that carried the Pilgrims to the New World in 1620 was a fairly small trading ship. She was about 90 feet (27 meters) long. That's about the length of six taxicabs lined up in a row. Some passengers on the "Mayflower" slept in bunks along the sides of the ship. Others made their beds on the floor of the covered deck. The upper part of the ship had many leaks. So the Pilgrims often felt ice-cold water splashing on them.

Before she carried passengers, the "Mayflower" had carried wine. So the ship's hold (the place where the cargo is kept) smelled quite sweet. Most ships of that time smelled of garbage and damp cargo.

The voyage of the "Mayflower" from England to Massachusetts took more than two months. Today you can fly the same distance on an SST airplane in three and a half hours!

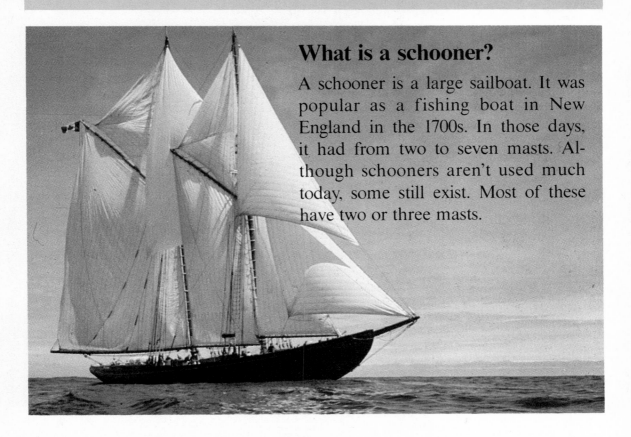

What is a schooner?

A schooner is a large sailboat. It was popular as a fishing boat in New England in the 1700s. In those days, it had from two to seven masts. Although schooners aren't used much today, some still exist. Most of these have two or three masts.

What does the word "schooner" mean?

The name "schooner" comes from a game that was popular when the schooner was first designed in 1713. Young boys used to throw flat stones in the bay and watch them skip along the water. They called this game "scooning." ("Scoon" is a Scottish word for "glide.") People say that when one of the new sailing boats first appeared, someone shouted, "See how she scoons!" The name stuck—even though the word is spelled differently today.

I FIND IT HARD TO BELIEVE THAT SKIPPING THOSE ROCKS CAN AMUSE YOU FOR HOURS ON END...

TYPICAL REACTION OF A NON "SCHOONER!"

63

What were the first ships to run on a regular schedule?

The first regularly scheduled ships were packet ships. These passenger ships became popular in the mid-1800s. Before this time, ships sailed only when conditions were right. They had to have full loads of both cargo and passengers. And the weather had to be good. Packet ships sailed at a set time no matter what! Their owners also made an effort to see to it that first-class passengers were comfortable. So, packet ships were popular with rich ocean travelers. No other shipowners had bothered much about passengers before.

What were the fastest sailing ships?

Clipper ships were the fastest and the most beautiful of the great sailing ships. Both their beauty and their speed came from the way they were built. They had long, sleek bodies and a large number of sails. Some clippers had as many as 35 sails.

Clipper ships were used during the mid-1800s. At that time the United States and East Asia (especially China) were doing a great deal of trading. Clippers carried tea, coffee, and spices. These things would spoil if they remained on board ship for too long a period of time. So speed was very important. Clipper ships were named for the way they could "clip off the miles." A clipper could make a trip from the east coast of the United States to China and back in six months. It had to travel all the way around the tip of South America to get to the Pacific Ocean. So six months was a record time in those days.

Were windjammers a kind of ship?

Yes, windjammers were iron sailing ships with four masts. They became popular just after clipper ships. They, too, were used for trading and carrying cargo from East Asia. Windjammers were huge and strong. They were perfect for sailing in bad weather and rough seas.

When did people start using steamboats?

The first workable steamboat was built in 1787 by an American named John Fitch. The boat had six long paddles on each side—like a big canoe! The paddles were moved by a steam engine.

Three years later, Fitch improved his model and put the paddles at the back. He then started taking passengers and cargo up and down the Delaware River. However, the engine was so large, there was very little room for the cargo. And not many people were interested in traveling on a steamboat. So Fitch's steamboat service failed.

What was "Fulton's Folly"?

In 1807 Robert Fulton built the "Clermont," the first successful steamboat. People thought that building a steamboat was a foolish idea. So they called the boat "Fulton's Folly." But building the "Clermont" turned out to be a smart idea—not a foolish one. Fulton had combined the best features from steamboats other people had invented. Before long, the "Clermont" was making regular trips along the Hudson River in New York.

"Clermont" on the Hudson River

What did the "Clermont" look like?

This is a picture of the "Clermont." Even though it had a bulky steam engine, the boat carried two masts with sails—just in case. It also had a smokestack that coughed out black smoke. It did not have canoe paddles like those on John Fitch's steamboat. Instead, the "Clermont" had a paddle wheel on each side.

66

Though the "Clermont" had room to seat 24 passengers, only 14 people were brave enough to go on its first trip. Yet one month later, 90 passengers crowded on board!

What is a paddle wheel?

A paddle wheel is a huge wheel with a series of flat paddles attached to it. On a moving steamboat, part of the wheel was always underwater. The power from a steam engine turned the wheel forward. As the paddles pushed against the water, they moved the boat forward.

What was a showboat?

A showboat was a paddle-wheel steamboat used as a traveling theater. In the 1800s, gaily decorated showboats brought plays, circuses, and live music to towns along the Mississippi River. Some boats even carried zoos and museums! Often the show was held right on the boat. But sometimes the showboat pulled a flat boat, called a barge, behind it. Then the theater was on the barge.

Why don't we see paddle-wheel boats any more?

Because the paddle wheel was replaced by the propeller. Starting in 1816, some steamboats used propellers. Others still had paddle wheels. Great arguments took place as to which was better. In 1845 two nearly identical British ships had a series of contests. The "Rattler" had a propeller. The "Alecto" had a paddle wheel. The "Rattler" won every race. Soon after that, propellers replaced paddle wheels. Propellers are still used on ships today.

Where were paddleboats used?

Mostly on rivers. There is less wind over a river than over an ocean. Therefore, sailboats move slowly on rivers. But steamboats can move quickly. In America steamboats became very popular on the great Mississippi and Ohio rivers.

"Savannah"

What was the first steamship to cross the Atlantic?

The paddle-wheeler "Savannah." In 1819 she left her home port in Georgia for Liverpool, England. Many people believed that such a "steam coffin" would never make it all the way across the Atlantic Ocean. But she did—29 days later.

Twenty-nine days was not a record time for a ship to cross the Atlantic. Any packet ship of the day could have made the trip in that amount of time—or even less. Why wasn't the trip faster? The "Savannah" was built as a sailing ship. Her steam engine and paddle wheels were added later. Most of the first Atlantic crossing was made using sail power. The "Savannah" had only enough fuel to run her engine for about 85 hours (less than four days). Her trip was a first—but only a small beginning for steam.

The first all-steam ship crossing took place 19 years later. The "Sirius" (SIR-ee-us) made the trip from Ireland to the east coast of the United States in 18½ days. By the 1840s many steamships were making trips across the Atlantic Ocean.

Do we still use steamships today?

Yes. You have probably seen pictures of huge ocean liners, like the "Queen Elizabeth 2." You may even have seen some of the actual liners. You can recognize them by their large smokestacks. Most ships with a smokestack are steamships. But some modern ships have diesel engines, and others are run by atomic energy.

How long does it take a steamship to cross the ocean today?

A fast steamship can cross the Atlantic Ocean between New York and Southampton, England, in 5½ days.

It takes about 12 days for a fast steamship to cross the Pacific Ocean from Seattle, Washington, to Kobe, Japan.

...AND FOR SHOW AND TELL I BROUGHT ALONG A PICTURE I TOOK OF THE Q.E. 2. Q.E. 2...THAT'S TRAVEL TALK FOR THE QUEEN ELIZABETH II.

70

Is a trip on a modern ocean liner any fun?

Yes! A modern ocean liner is like a floating hotel. Once on board, it's easy to forget you're on a ship. The rooms are something like hotel rooms. And every modern convenience is right at your fingertips. There are restaurants, shops, game rooms, elevators, theaters, gymnasiums, and swimming pools. Some liners even have tennis courts!

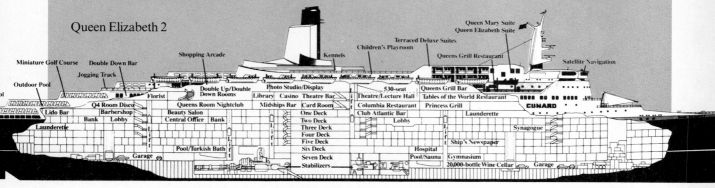

Queen Elizabeth 2

What's the difference between a port and a harbor?

Sometimes people use the words "port" and "harbor" to mean the same thing. But there is a difference. All ports are harbors, but not all harbors are ports.

A harbor is part of a body of water that is deep enough for anchoring boats or ships. It is partly surrounded by land. Or else it has man-made piers that stick out into the water. The land or the piers protect boats from strong winds and rough water currents.

A port is a special kind of harbor. Passengers and freight can be loaded or unloaded there. A large, busy port usually has cranes for handling heavy freight, warehouses for storing things, radio equipment, repair services, fueling stations, and even restaurants.

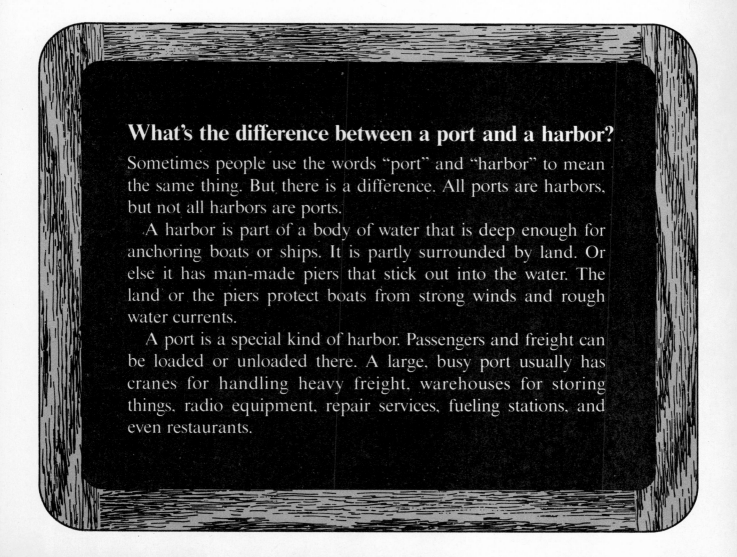

What is a cargo ship?

A cargo ship carries goods for trading. The old clipper ships were cargo ships. They carried tea and spices from China to America. They needed to be fast so that the cargo would not spoil before it could be unloaded. Today many cargo ships have refrigerators on them. So there is no spoilage problem.

Modern cargo ships are divided into four categories, according to the things they carry. General cargo ships carry things that are put in packages, such as food, machinery, and clothing. Tankers carry oil or other liquids. Dry bulk carriers carry unpackaged goods like coal or grain. Multipurpose ships carry a few different kinds of cargo at once.

How are cargo ships loaded and unloaded?

Large electric cranes lift boxes and barrels onto and off of general cargo ships. Once the cargo is aboard, crew members store it in various places in the ship.

Some general cargo ships called container ships carry all the cargo in large, weatherproof metal boxes. Container ships are the quickest to load and unload. Cranes drop the boxes directly into special compartments on the ship where the boxes fit neatly. So, few crew members are needed to do the job. Later, each box is put on the trailer part of a tractor-trailer truck. Or else it is loaded right onto a railroad flatcar.

Oil is pumped on and off a tanker through special hoses.

What's a supertanker?

A supertanker is a very large oil-carrying tanker. It is the largest kind of non-military ship that exists. Picture three football fields in a row. Many supertankers are longer even than that! Supertankers are slower than other types of large ships. But they provide the cheapest way to carry oil.

73

What is a tramp ship?

Like a person we call a tramp, a tramp ship travels around looking for any work it can find. Most cargo ships carry their loads on a regular schedule and over a special route. A tramp ship is a cargo ship with no fixed schedule or route. It travels from port to port, taking whatever work is available. It goes wherever cargo needs to be taken.

What is a harbor pilot?

When a ship comes into or leaves a port, a harbor pilot must be on board. His job is to guide the ship through the harbor waters. The pilot must be familiar with the tides, the winds, and all the markers in the harbor's waters. The markers tell the pilot where the water is shallow or where there are dangerous rocks.

What do tugboats do?

Tugboats are small, powerful boats. They are used to tow and guide bigger boats and ships into or out of a harbor. Most tugs are used to pull large ocean liners and cargo ships through shallow waters or narrow areas. Without the tugs, large ships have a hard time moving through such places. Some tugs tow damaged ships into the harbor.

Modern tugboats get their power from diesel engines, like the ones used in locomotives. But in the 1800s, tugs were driven by steam-powered paddle wheels.

What does a fireboat do?

A fireboat puts out fires on ships and piers. Most big ports have at least one fireboat. It is equipped with powerful "water guns" that shoot great streams of water at the fire. A nozzle at the top of a tall tower shoots water the farthest. It can aim water at the deck or the inside of a burning ship. When big passenger liners come into the harbor, fireboats sometimes greet them by spraying water high into the air.

76

What is a dry dock?

In order for a ship to be repaired and painted, it must be taken out of the water. Since large ships are heavy, special docks called dry docks were invented for the purpose. There are two main kinds—the floating dock and the graving dock.

The floating dry dock is a floating platform with walls on two sides. Water is pumped into it. The dock sinks, and the ship moves onto it. When the water is pumped out again, the dock rises once more to the surface. Now the ship is in dry dock.

The graving dry dock is a deep concrete tub sunk into the ground. One end of it opens into the harbor. When the ship enters, a gate closes it off from the harbor. Then water is pumped out. The ship sinks with the water. When all the water has been pumped out, the ship is in dry dock.

What is a barge?

A barge is a flat-bottomed boat used to carry heavy freight, like coal or steel. It usually has square ends that make docking and unloading easy.

In the old days, barges had no motors. They were pulled by horses or oxen. The animals would walk on the land next to the river or canal, pulling ropes attached to the barge. (Now this towing work is usually done by other boats.) Some modern barges have their own motors. These barges can carry up to 20 million pounds (9 million kilograms), of freight.

What kind of boat is a ferry?

A ferry is a boat that carries passengers across a small body of water, like a lake or a river. Some ferries carry people across even larger bodies of water. However, all ferries travel back and forth between two ports on a regular schedule. Some ferry rides take five minutes. Others take two days. The ferries that make long trips have dining rooms and sleeping compartments.

Ferries often carry more than passengers. Some are large enough to carry cars or even railroad trains.

Most ferries are run by diesel or steam engines. But in some places, you can find ferries that are pushed along with poles. Others are pulled by men or animals on a nearby shore or river bank.

! ! ! !

Ferries that carry trains across a body of water have their own tracks. So a whole train can ride right onto a train ferry and then ride off again!

What are gondolas?

Gondolas are long, thin rowboats often used as water taxis. They are popular in Venice, Italy. Instead of roads, most of Venice has canals—narrow inland waterways. So people there use boats instead of cars to travel from place to place.

At the back of a gondola stands the gondolier—the man who runs the boat. He uses a long, narrow pole to push his gondola through the shallow canals.

Is a junk a rotten old boat?

No. A junk is a kind of wooden sailboat. It was first used by the Chinese a few hundred years ago. If you go to the Orient today, you will still see many junks. They are usually painted in bright colors. White circles on the front stand for eyes. They are the boats' guiding spirits that watch for dangers.

Junks have flat bottoms and high sterns (backs). They have two or more four-cornered sails. Compared to modern boats, junks are slow and hard to handle. That's why some people have put outboard motors on their junks.

Junk

79

What is a catamaran?

A catamaran is a sailboat made by joining two separate hulls together. A little space is left between them. "Cats," as these strange-looking boats are called, are very fast. The two hulls give them excellent balance.

Catamarans were invented by people who lived in the South Seas—a part of the Pacific Ocean. There the natives used logs to make the two hulls. They used paddles and sometimes added sails to make their cats move. The South Sea natives used catamarans to carry things over long distances. Some people still use catamarans today.

What is a sampan?

A sampan is a small, fast-moving boat found in China, Japan, and other nearby countries. A sampan is often used as a house for a family. Some sampans are also used for carrying things to be sold.

Not all sampans look alike. But most have a cabin that is covered with straw mats. The cabin is where people usually sleep. Most sampans have oars and sails. If there's no wind for sailing, the owners can always row.

Where is there a floating sampan "city"?

In Hong Kong, a British colony on the south coast of China. Here groups of people live or work on sampans, docked one right next to the other. Some sampans are homes. Others are food stores or restaurants. Many of the sampans are very old. Their cabin covers are full of patches.

Sampan

Catamaran

TERORO

Sampan City

Do any people in the U.S. live on boats?

Some Americans live on floating homes called houseboats. Houseboats don't usually have power of their own. To travel from one place to another, they have to be towed by a second boat. Some families in the warmer parts of the United States live on houseboats all year round. Other people rent houseboats just for the summer months or for an even shorter period of time. Still others spend their summers on yachts.

The largest private sailing yacht ever built was the "Sea Cloud." It was owned by Mrs. Marjorie Merriweather Post, a very wealthy woman. The "Sea Cloud" was 350 feet (105 meters) long —longer even than the largest sailing ships ever built!

What is a yacht?

A yacht is any kind of large boat used for pleasure cruising. It can be a graceful sailboat or a streamlined powerboat.

What do sailing yachts look like?

Here are the pictures of three sailing yachts—a yawl, a ketch, and a schooner. These all have two masts and three or more sails. Most yachts are longer than 5 taxicabs in a row. Some are even longer than 20 taxicabs in a row!

Ketch   Schooner   Yawl

83

How did sailing ships help to celebrate America's 200th birthday?

Two hundred twenty-six sailing ships from all over the world came to New York City on July 4, 1976, and paraded up the Hudson River. The parade was called Operation Sail 1976, or Op Sail '76. It was part of America's 200th birthday celebration.

Only 20 tall sailing ships with square sails were left in the world at that time. Sixteen of them took part in Op Sail. So did 60 naval ships from 40 countries, and 150 other large ships. Thousands of small boats sailed into the Hudson so their owners could watch the parade. Many thousands of people watched from windows and along the river's edge.

85

What makes a boat float?

When something solid, like a boat, is put into a liquid, like water, the solid pushes some of the liquid aside. If the solid weighs more than the liquid it pushes aside, it will sink. If it weighs less, it will float. A huge, heavy ship floats, too, even though it is made of steel. A big ship contains lots of air, so it weighs less than the water it pushes aside. That is why it floats.

Why are most boats long and narrow?

Long, narrow boats can go through the water quickly. A force called "drag" holds back anything that moves through water. The wider the boat, the more "drag" there is to hold it back. So a long, thin boat can go faster. A boat shaped to get the least possible drag from the water is said to be "streamlined."

Do all boats need anchors?

Yes, unless they are tied to a dock. An anchor is a heavy metal object attached to a boat by a long rope. When the anchor is thrown overboard, its pointed hook digs into the bottom of the ocean or the lake. It keeps the boat from drifting away. Before leaving a boat, a good sailor pulls on the anchor, to make sure it has a firm hold in the ground.

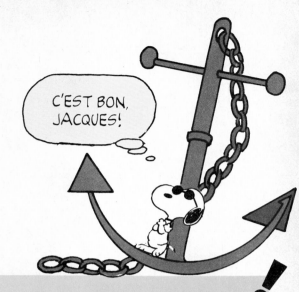

C'EST BON, JACQUES!

The famous ocean scientist Jacques Cousteau (ZHOCK koo-STOE) sank an anchor 24,600 feet (about 7,400 meters) into the Atlantic Ocean!

Jacques Cousteau's research ship, the "Calypso"

What do "knots" mean to a sailor?

Instead of giving speed in "miles per hour" or "kilometers per hour," sailors refer to "knots." A knot equals 1.15 miles per hour. To change from miles per hour to knots, divide by 1.15. For example, 38 miles per hour is the same as 33 knots.

ships captains keep logs to burn in the furnace if the weather gets cold.

I FEEL I'M ABOUT TO BE DRAWN INTO A HEATED DISCUSSION!

Why do ships' captains keep logs?

Sally is thinking of the wrong kind of log. A ship's log is the daily record of a trip. The ship's captain is usually the one who keeps the log. The captain writes down all the important details of the trip. These include the exact route, events that happen on board, and radio messages. Over the years, ships' logs have been a great help in piecing together facts about the history of sea travel. A log is also important if a ship has an accident. It helps uncover the reason for the mishap or disaster.

Do ships' captains have road maps to follow?

Yes, in a way. A ship's captain has the help of one or more specially trained people called navigators. Before beginning a voyage, the navigators mark the ship's route on a special sea map, called a chart. During the trip, they keep track of the ship's position by using radar and other electronic equipment. The captain uses this information to stay on the course marked on the chart.

In ancient times, sailors figured out their direction by looking at the stars. Of course, they were in trouble if the sky was cloudy. By the 1100s, sailors were using compasses to tell direction. Today, navigation is much easier. Modern ships rarely get lost at sea.

Section of nautical chart of the Hudson River

How does a compass work?

A compass needle is a magnet. So are the earth's North and South poles. If a compass needle is free to turn, it lines itself up with the earth's magnetic poles. One end points toward the north. The other end points toward the south.

Letters painted on a dial under the needle show all the directions. A sailor just has to look at the compass to see which way the ship is going. For example, if the north end of the compass needle points toward the back of the ship, that means north is behind it. The ship is traveling south.

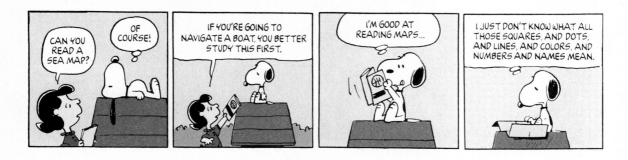

How does radar help ships?

The word "radar" stands for **ra**dio **d**etecting **a**nd **r**anging. It is a way of telling direction and distance by using radio waves. A radar antenna sends out, in all directions, special signals called radio waves. When these waves bump into a solid object, they bounce back to the antenna. The radar device measures the time it takes for the waves to travel back and forth. Then it figures out where the object is.

Radar will warn a ship's captain—even in a fog—of something in the way of the ship.

89

What is a buoy?

A buoy (BOO-ee) is a specially shaped or marked float that helps a sailor get around in strange waters. Most buoys are used as channel markers. They warn sailors of shallow or rocky areas or give them other important information. There are also some types of buoys used for mooring (tying up) a boat.

Do any boats move along on the surface of the water?

Two kinds of boats move along on the water's surface—hydrofoils and hovercraft. A hydrofoil skims very quickly over the water. Its hull, or bottom, is just above the surface. Only the hydrofoil's "sea wings" stay in the water. These work very much like airplane wings. When a plane picks up speed, the wings lift it into the air. In the same way, when the hydrofoil picks up speed, its sea wings lift it out of the water. When the boat is in this position, there is less drag from the water. So the hydrofoil can travel much faster than other kinds of boats. Hydrofoils are used for passenger travel and by the military.

Hovercraft—also called air-cushioned vehicles (ACVs)—can be driven on water or land. They have fans or propellers that take in air at the top and blow it out the bottom. A hovercraft is lifted above the surface of the water by the air that comes out under it. These amazing vehicles shouldn't really be called "boats," since they travel above the surface of the water, not in it. Hovercraft can go almost anywhere—swamps, mud, river rapids, ice.

Hydrofoil

What is an iceboat?

An iceboat is a narrow, pointed sailboat that travels on ice instead of on water. It can do this because it rests on runners—usually three. They look something like short skis. An iceboat's sails are usually very large. They catch the wind and make the iceboat move ahead—just as they would on any sailboat.

Iceboating (also called iceyachting) has long been a favorite pastime in Norway, Sweden, Denmark, and Finland. There the water is frozen most of the year. Today it is a popular winter sport in many other countries as well, including the United States and Canada.

 An iceboat can move twice as fast as the wind!

I ALWAYS THOUGHT AN ICEBREAKER MEANT SOMEONE WHO COULD LIVEN UP A DULL PARTY!

Can any kind of ship travel through frozen waters?

An icebreaker is a special kind of ship designed to break through ice. Its front section, or bow, is covered with strong metal which acts as armor. Its engines are very powerful. It also has propellers both in back and in front. They make the ship easier to handle than an ordinary ship. To break the ice, the ship's bow climbs partly up on the ice. Its weight causes the ice to break.

91

U.S. Coast Guard Icebreakers

Has any ship ever sailed to the North Pole?

No ship has ever reached the North Pole on the surface of the water. Ice stops most ships. But one kind of ship can avoid the ice: the submarine, because it moves underwater. In 1958 the nuclear submarine "Nautilus" reached the North Pole by traveling underneath the ice. The next year another nuclear submarine, the "Skate," broke through the North Pole ice.

How does a submarine go up and down?

In order to dive, or go down, a submarine takes water into special storage tanks. The water adds weight to the sub. When the sub gets heavy enough, it sinks. To surface, or go up, air is forced into the tanks to blow out the water. The submarine rises to the surface of the sea. It will stay on the surface until the tanks are flooded with water again.

Once under water, a sub can move upward or downward by using steel fins at the rear of the ship. These are called diving planes. When the fins are tilted down, the submarine will dive. When they are tilted up, the sub will move upward.

How else are submarines used?

Oceanographers (o-she-uh-NOG-ruh-furz)—scientists who study ocean life—use submarines to explore the bottom of the sea. They also use submarines to enable them to get valuable minerals from the ocean floor. Small submarines, called submersibles, are used to explore sunken ships.

What were the first submarines like?

Early submarine experiments date back hundreds of years. In the 1620s, a Dutch engineer built a leather-covered rowing boat that could travel underwater. Twelve men with oars sat inside and rowed. The inventor, Cornelius Drebbel, used some sort of chemical to keep the air breathable. But he kept the formula a secret. So no one knows what it was.

The first submarine ever used in a war was called the "Turtle." It was built and used in 1776 during the American Revolution. It attacked a British warship. But the attack was not successful. The ship did not sink.

The "Turtle" was well named. It was shaped something like a turtle's shell. A man sat inside, turning a pole called a crankshaft. The crankshaft was attached to propellers. When the crankshaft moved, the propellers moved. When the propellers moved, the sub moved.

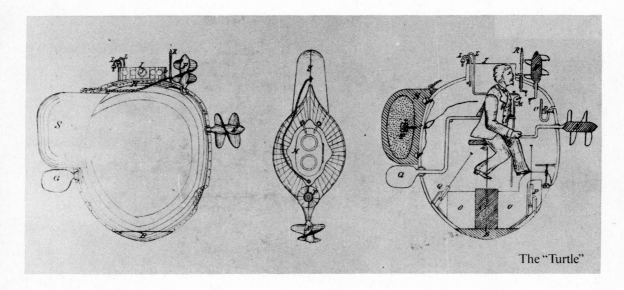

The "Turtle"

How did later submarines solve the air problem?

In the early 1900s, submarines could stay underwater for only short periods of time. The subs did not have any way to replace air. The problem was solved with a snorkel. This is a tube that came out the top of the sub. It allowed fresh air to come into the cabin and to cool the engines. With snorkels, subs could travel for long periods just below the surface of the water. But they could not stay in deep water for more than a few hours at a time.

From sea water, modern submarines can make their own oxygen—the gas we take from the air when we breathe. So the length of time subs can stay underwater does not depend on air supply.

What kind of power do submarines use today?

Modern submarines use nuclear energy. It is the most powerful force known. Uranium (you-RAY-nee-um) is the fuel used for nuclear energy. One ounce (28 grams) of it gives out as much energy as the burning of 100 tons (90 metric tons) of coal. So nuclear-powered subs can travel long distances without refueling.

Are any ships besides submarines powered by nuclear energy?

Yes. Nuclear energy has been used in a few U.S. and Russian ships. But nuclear power for ships is still in the experimental stage. The equipment needed is very bulky. And it's also very expensive. That's why most ships today are powered by diesel or steam engines.

 The "U.S.S. Enterprise," a nuclear-powered ship, can travel more than 200,000 miles (320,000 kilometers) without refueling. That's about eight times around the world!

What's the deepest anyone ever has gone in the ocean?

Nearly 36,000 feet (10,800 meters). Since the 16th century, scientists have used diving bells—round, airtight containers—to go under water. Until recently, these bells were lowered into the water on heavy ropes or steel cables. In 1960, two men went down 35,817 feet (10,745 meters) into the Pacific Ocean. They reached the deepest known part of the ocean. The long trip down took more than five hours. The divers were in a bathyscaphe (BATH-ih-skafe). This is a modern diving bell used to explore the ocean. The bathyscaphe carries heavy steel to make it sink. When the steel is dropped, the bathyscaphe gets lighter so it comes up again. Bathyscaphes carry oxygen in bottles and also chemicals for cleaning used air.

A Bathyscaphe being lowered into the water.

Charlie Brown in the Air

RIGHT ON!

WING POWER

How did people first try to fly?

People made wings of feathers and tried to fly like birds. They attached their homemade wings to their arms and jumped from high places. Usually they were killed or badly injured.

In 1490, an Italian named Danti made some wings. For a moment it looked as if they would work. But Danti crashed to the ground. He was seriously hurt.

John Damian lived in Scotland. He made wings of feathers, too. In 1507, he jumped from the top of a castle. He fell and broke his leg.

Wan Ho lived in China in about 1500. He was very brave. He tried to rocket through space. He tied 47 rockets to the back of his chair. Then he strapped himself in. Some friends attached two kites to his chair. They lit the rockets. There was a great big explosion and lots of smoke. Wan Ho was never seen again.

Who is Icarus?

Icarus is the unfortunate hero of an ancient Greek story. His father made wings of feathers for him. The feathers were glued together with wax. "Be careful," warned his father. "Don't fly too near the sun or the wax will melt." But according to the legend, Icarus didn't listen to his father. Instead, he flew near the warm rays of the sun and the wax melted. Feathers fell from Icarus' wings, and he plunged into the sea and drowned.

What was the first successful flying machine?

The first successful flying machine was a balloon built by Joseph and Jacques Montgolfier (ZHOCK mawn-gawl-FYAY) in 1782. The brothers were watching a fire burning in their fireplace. They noticed that the smoke went up the chimney. They watched other fires and saw that smoke always went up. The brothers wondered why. They decided that there must be something special about smoke. Joseph and Jacques trapped some smoke in a paper bag. It was a risky thing to do. The bag could have caught fire. But it didn't. It floated in the air.

On June 5, they took a bag that measured 35 feet (11 meters) around. It weighed 300 pounds (135 kilograms). The brothers made a smoky fire by burning straw. They floated the bag over the fire. It rose more than a mile (almost 2 kilometers) high before it cooled off and came back down. This was the first balloon flight.

Later, people discovered that it was heat and not smoke that made balloons rise.

The first Montgolfier balloon

How does the hot-air balloon work?

A hot-air balloon is a large, airtight cloth or plastic bag filled with heated air. Hot air is lighter than cool air. So hot air rises. The hot air inside the balloon is lighter than the cool air outside, so the balloon rises. When the heated air cools and becomes as heavy as the air outside, the balloon will stop rising and come down.

A balloon carries heavy weights in a basket that is tied to its bottom end. The weights are usually bags of sand. When the weights are thrown out, the balloon starts to rise. As more and more weights are thrown out, the balloon rises higher. When the passengers want to come down, they can open the top of the bag to let out heated air.

Hot-air balloons are open at the bottom. They are filled with hot air by lighting a gas burner underneath the opening. Today most balloons are not filled with hot air. Gases that are lighter than air are used instead. Helium is a lighter-than-air gas that is often used.

Early balloons carried sponges and a bucket of water for putting out the fires that kept starting!

THAT'S MY SISTER LUCY. SHE LOVES TO MAKE A GRAND ENTRANCE!

99

Who was the first person to fly?

Pilâtre de Rozier (pee-LAH-truh duh raw-ZYAY) of France was the first person to fly. A duck, a sheep, and a rooster had already flown in a Montgolfier balloon. Now it was man's turn. King Louis XVI (the sixteenth) offered to send up a prisoner who was supposed to die soon. But de Rozier begged to go instead.

On October 15, 1783, Pilâtre de Rozier climbed aboard the balloon. It rose 80 feet (24 meters) into the air, about as high as a six-story building. It probably would have gone higher, but it was held down by a rope. Man's first flight lasted 4½ minutes. The balloon weighed 1,600 pounds (more than 700 kilograms).

How fast can a balloon go?

A balloon has no moving power of its own. It can travel only as fast as the wind that carries it.

Why did people stop using balloons for travel?

Balloon flight can't be controlled. Some people tried to steer balloons by using sails. Others tried oars. A few people tried paddles. Nothing worked. When better airships were invented, people lost interest in balloons.

How are balloons used today?

Scientists use very big plastic balloons to gather weather information. Balloons carry equipment to record temperature, humidity (moisture), air pressure, and wind speeds. This information is sent back to the scientists by radio equipment carried by the balloons.

If a weather balloon breaks, the instruments it carries float back to earth in a bright red parachute.

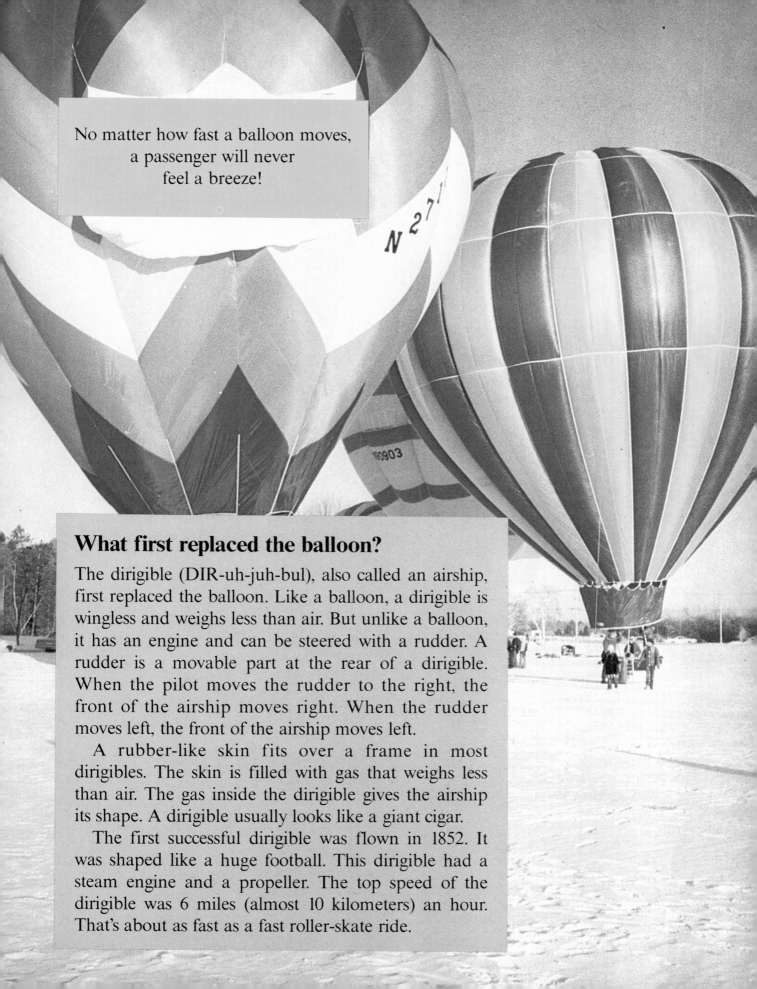

No matter how fast a balloon moves, a passenger will never feel a breeze!

What first replaced the balloon?

The dirigible (DIR-uh-juh-bul), also called an airship, first replaced the balloon. Like a balloon, a dirigible is wingless and weighs less than air. But unlike a balloon, it has an engine and can be steered with a rudder. A rudder is a movable part at the rear of a dirigible. When the pilot moves the rudder to the right, the front of the airship moves right. When the rudder moves left, the front of the airship moves left.

A rubber-like skin fits over a frame in most dirigibles. The skin is filled with gas that weighs less than air. The gas inside the dirigible gives the airship its shape. A dirigible usually looks like a giant cigar.

The first successful dirigible was flown in 1852. It was shaped like a huge football. This dirigible had a steam engine and a propeller. The top speed of the dirigible was 6 miles (almost 10 kilometers) an hour. That's about as fast as a fast roller-skate ride.

A zeppelin

What was a zeppelin?

A zeppelin was a large dirigible. It was named for the man who designed it, Count Ferdinand von Zeppelin of Germany.

The first zeppelin was built in 1900. It had a cigar-shaped aluminum frame. It weighed 25,350 pounds (11,408 kilograms), about as much as two large male elephants.

How were zeppelins used?

Zeppelins carried passengers who wanted to go sightseeing. Regularly scheduled zeppelin trips flew across the Atlantic Ocean. Count von Zeppelin began an airline company that carried 34,288 people in four years without an accident. During World War I zeppelins had another use. One hundred zeppelins were built for war. Their mission—bombing London!

In 1928 the Graf Zeppelin flew around the world in 22 days!

"AROUND THE WORLD IN 22 DAYS"...I WONDER IF I COULD WRITE A SONG ABOUT THAT??!

What was the Hindenburg?

The Hindenburg was the largest airship ever built. It was a zeppelin 803 feet (241 meters) long. That's about as long as 54 taxis in a line. The Hindenburg was 135 feet (more than 40 meters) wide. That's about as long as 9 taxis in a line. The Hindenburg had a lounge, a piano, and paneled bedrooms. It made 35 trips across the Atlantic Ocean. On May 6, 1937, it suddenly exploded and burned as it was trying to land at Lakehurst, New Jersey. There were 97 people aboard. Thirty-six of them died. No one ever found out what caused the disaster. But zeppelins were filled with hydrogen gas, which people knew was very explosive. After the Hindenburg tragedy, hydrogen was never used in airships again. And zeppelins were never again manufactured.

The Hindenburg

Will zeppelins ever be used again?

Perhaps zeppelins will be used again in the future. Scientists today are beginning to think about lighter-than-air aircraft once again. A zeppelin, powered by the most powerful energy in the world—atomic energy—might work well. Atomic energy uses very little fuel. An atomic zeppelin would not have to be refueled very often. It could remain in the air for a week at a time. Zeppelins can stay still in the sky. A zeppelin could remain in one place while scientists studied the land and water below. Some people are sure that zeppelins will make a comeback.

What is a blimp used for?

There are only two blimps in existence today. They are owned by the Goodyear Rubber Company. They are used for advertising. You can't help noticing a Goodyear Blimp when it cruises in the sky.

Blimps are small dirigibles. They are usually filled with helium gas. Blimp is a nickname. The first model was called an A-Limp. The B-Limp was an improved ship. Later its name was shortened to blimp.

When was the parachute invented?

No one knows exactly when the parachute was invented. The idea for what we now call a parachute is a very old one.

Chin Shih Huang Ti (cheen shur hoo-WANG DEE) ruled China about 2,100 years ago. He liked to jump from the Great Wall of China carrying an open umbrella over his head. The umbrella slowed the emperor's fall. He was never hurt.

Sébastien Lenormand (say-bah-STYAN luh-nor-MAWN) built a 14-foot (4-meter) chute. He used it in 1783, to jump from a tower. He claimed he had just invented a way of escaping from burning apartment houses. A few years later, daring balloonists began doing stunts with parachutes. Sometimes they carried parachutes just for protection in case their balloons burst into flames.

How does a parachute work?

An open parachute looks like a big umbrella. As a parachute falls to earth, the air underneath pushes upward against it. This push slows its fall. The umbrella part is attached to long lines. The lines are attached to straps around the jumper's body. The parachute is folded up in a small pack. It is strapped to the jumper's back. When the jumper leaps into the air, usually from an airplane, he or she pulls a string called the ripcord. That makes the parachute open. Sometimes the ripcord is hooked to a line inside the plane. In this case, when the jumper jumps out, the ripcord is pulled automatically. The rushing air fills the chute out into its umbrella shape and slows it down. Even so, the jumper hits the ground at about 15 miles (24 kilometers) an hour. It's a lot like jumping from a moving car.

Sometimes parachutes are attached to the tails of big, fast airplanes. The parachutes pop out behind the airplanes. This helps to slow the planes down when they are landing. Parachutes also pop out and help to slow down spacecraft returning to earth.

I'M AFRAID TO LOOK!... I SURE HOPE HIS INSURANCE COVERS THIS SORT OF THING!!

What is skydiving?

Skydiving is a popular modern sport. Skydivers carry parachutes and jump from planes that are often as high as 12,500 feet (3,750 meters) in the air. Skydivers do stunts in the sky for about a minute before they open their parachutes. They do loops, turns, barrel rolls, and more. Sometimes a group of skydivers will join hands and form a circle.

Skydivers open their parachutes when they are no less than 2,500 feet (750 meters) above the ground. They float to earth at 12 miles (about 19 kilometers) an hour. Skydiving is the fastest-growing sport in America.

 Before skydivers open their parachutes, they can float through the air at 200 miles (320 kilometers) an hour! That's nearly four times as fast as a car on a highway!

How does a glider plane fly?

A glider is an airplane without an engine. It is usually towed up into the air by an engine-powered airplane. The two are connected by a tow rope. When the rope is released, the glider flies through currents of rising air. The air pushes the glider up. The currents may be warm air rising from hot, flat areas of the earth. Or they may be wind currents that have been turned upward after hitting a hillside.

Without the air currents, called "updrafts," the motorless glider would settle down to earth. Even the biggest engine-powered airplanes act like gliders when they come in for a landing.

What is hang gliding?

Hang gliding is a popular American sport. The person gliding wears a harness which is attached to a glider. The glider looks something like a huge kite. It is shaped like a triangle. At its widest point, a glider is about as wide as a car is long. The pilot holds on to the glider and races down a hill into the wind. Or else the pilot jumps off a cliff. The wind lifts the glider into the air. The pilot uses a control bar to change directions. A hang glider usually travels as fast as a car would travel on a busy street. A person learning to hang glide usually flies 10–20 feet (3–6 meters) above the earth. That's about as high as a one-story building. After a while an experienced pilot may take the glider up higher. Hang gliders never fly as high as airplanes.

Orville Wright

Wilbur Wright

Who invented the airplane?

The Wright Brothers invented the first safe, successful airplane. But their first flight, on December 17, 1903, was not great news. Nothing appeared in the newspapers on that day. A few days later, short items began to appear in newspapers across the country, but no one seemed very interested or impressed.

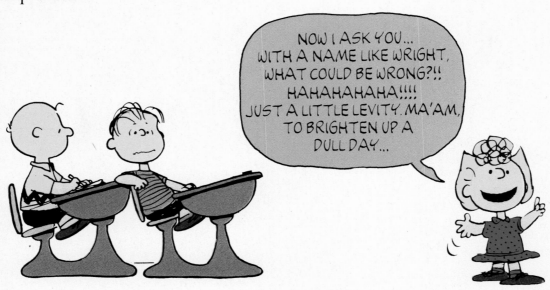

How long did the first airplane flight last?

Orville Wright took the "Flyer I" up in the air and flew it for 12 seconds. Wilbur Wright took turns with his brother flying their airplane. The next two flights lasted twice as long as the first one. On the fourth flight that day, the airplane stayed in the air for 59 seconds. After it landed, a sudden gust of wind tipped the plane over. "Flyer I" was badly damaged. The first successful airplane was never flown again.

Wright Brothers' take off

Some people say "Flyer I" never got off the ground. The Wright Brothers had no witnesses to prove that the plane flew!

Who was the first person to fly across the sea?

Louis Blériot (loo-EE blay-RYO) flew across the English Channel in 1909. He flew from France to England in a Blériot XI (eleven) monoplane. A monoplane has only one set of wings. Most early planes had two sets—one above the other.

Blériot's flight was historic. He proved that people from different countries could now visit each other fairly easily.

Blériot monoplane

Who was the first woman pilot?

Baroness de la Roche (duh lah RAWSH) was the first woman pilot. She made her first flight in 1908. Two years later, Baroness de la Roche received a pilot's license.

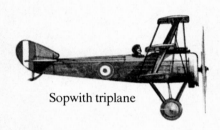
Sopwith triplane

Nieuport 28

Nieuport 17

How were planes first used to help fight a war?

Airplanes were first used for war in October 1911. During the Italo-Turkish War, an Italian pilot flew over enemy lands. He wanted to see what the enemy was doing. The first bombing raid came a few days later. An Italian pilot dropped four grenades over Turkish lands. He also scattered leaflets in the air. The leaflets urged the people to surrender.

Albatros D.3

Fokker D.8

What are dogfights?

Dogfights are airplane sky battles. They were common during World War I, which began in 1914. Squadrons of 10 to 20 planes fought each other in the sky. The planes twisted and turned in many directions as each pilot tried to shoot the enemy. A pilot would try to get behind an enemy plane before firing his guns. This kept him safe from bullets, but close enough to hit the enemy.

111

What was barnstorming?

Barnstorming was a type of show that stunt pilots gave in the early days of airplanes. Barnstorming pilots flew their planes from small town to small town, stopping wherever a fair or festival was going on. A pilot caught people's attention by performing daring acrobatic stunts and swooping low over the town and nearby farms. Airplanes were an unusual sight. So crowds soon gathered to watch the pilot's daring feats. Then the pilot landed his plane in a field and sold tickets for rides in the plane. Usually a quick air tour around the town cost five dollars.

The famous pilot Charles Lindbergh got his start in 1922 by helping barnstorming pilots attract crowds. Lindbergh performed parachute jumps and walked on the wings of flying planes!

112

What made Charles Lindbergh famous?

Charles Lindbergh was the first person to fly alone across the Atlantic Ocean. Raymond Orteig, a New York City hotel owner, offered $25,000 to the first person to fly nonstop from New York to Paris. Charles Lindbergh wanted to be that person.

On May 20, 1927, Lindbergh took off early in the morning from Garden City, New York. He flew his plane, the "Spirit of St. Louis," through fog, rain, and sleet. He landed in Paris 33 hours and 30 minutes later. He had flown 3,600 miles (nearly 5,800 kilometers).

"Spirit of St. Louis"

Where can you see the "Spirit of St. Louis"?

You can see Lindbergh's airplane at the National Air and Space Museum in Washington, D.C. After Lindbergh made his famous flight to Paris, he sent the "Spirit" back to the United States on a Navy ship. He flew it on a victory tour of Latin America. Then he flew the "Spirit" to Washington and gave it to the Smithsonian Institution. At the National Air and Space Museum, which is a branch of the Smithsonian, you can see not only the "Spirit of St. Louis," but also the Wright brothers' "Flyer" and many other famous airplanes and spacecraft.

What is a "flying ace"?

A flying ace is a pilot who has shot down five or more enemy planes.

Who was the Red Baron?

The Red Baron was Baron von Richthofen (RIKHT-hoe-fun) of Germany. He shot down 80 planes during World War I. That made him the greatest flying ace of all time. He was called the Red Baron because his plane was colored red. Sometimes he was known as the Red Knight. His flying squadron was known as Richthofen's Flying Circus.

Who was Amelia Earhart?

Amelia Earhart was a famous pilot. She was the first woman to travel as an airplane passenger across the Atlantic Ocean. She was also the first woman—and the second pilot—to fly across the Atlantic alone. To prepare for this long solo flight, she practiced going without sleep or food for many days at a time. Her flight from Newfoundland to Ireland took only about 14 hours. Amelia Earhart won many awards for her flying, including the Distinguished Flying Cross.

What finally happened to Amelia Earhart?

In 1937, she and Fred Noonan tried to fly a twin-engine airplane around the world. A ship picked up a radio signal from their airplane. They were short of fuel over the Pacific Ocean. Carrier planes and ships searched for them. No trace of Amelia Earhart, Fred Noonan, or their plane was ever found.

When did people start using airplanes to deliver the mail?

Some early airplane pilots and balloonists carried mail as a stunt. But the first official United States air-mail delivery was made in 1911, by Paul Beck and Earle Ovington. They delivered mail from Garden City, New York, to Jamaica, New York. This was a distance of less than 8 miles (almost 13 kilometers).

May 15, 1917, was the beginning of the first continuous air-mail service in the world. Army pilots flew military mail from different cities in Europe to New York City, Philadelphia, and Washington, D.C. Regular air-mail service from the United States to Europe began in 1918.

Today almost all mail that travels more than 100 miles (160 kilometers) goes by air.

! On an average day, Kennedy International Airport in New York handles ten million five hundred thousand (10,500,000) air-mail letters! !

HOW NICE... AN AIR MAIL LETTER!

What do bush pilots do?

Bush pilots fly to areas where very few people live. These areas are usually on mountains or in jungles or near the North and South poles. Bush pilots deliver food, medicine, and supplies. They take sick people to hospitals. Flying conditions are often dangerous. Winds near the poles may gust up to 100 miles (160 kilometers) an hour. Isolated areas usually don't have weather stations. So weather information is often not available. Neither are airports or landing fields, much of the time. Bush pilots sometimes have to land on ice. If the ice is too thin, the bush pilot is in trouble.

Bush pilots performed heroic deeds in the early days of flying. But today fewer regions are isolated. So the need for bush pilots is fast disappearing.

How can someone become an airplane pilot?

Every pilot has to have a license in order to fly an airplane. A person must be at least 16 years old to get a student's license, and 17 years old to get a regular license. Flying lessons are necessary, and they are expensive, too. They cost at least $600 a course. In the United States, the Federal Aviation Administration issues pilots' licenses. But first a student must pass a written test, a flying test, and an examination by a doctor.

There are many things to learn about flying. Students usually take courses in weather, air science, and the rules of flying.

A student pilot must spend at least 40 hours flying. A student learns to fly by watching an experienced pilot. He or she also learns by reading air charts and by studying the instruments on the plane. The student must complete one 100-mile (160-kilometer) flight without having the instructor in the plane.

What was the smallest airplane ever built?

The smallest airplane was the Stits Skybaby. It was built by Ray Stits in 1952. The Skybaby was about half as long as an average car.

What was the biggest airplane ever built?

The biggest airplane ever built was the H.2 "Hercules" flying boat. It measured 320 feet (96 meters) from wing tip to wing tip. It was 219 feet (66 meters) long, which is about 20 times as big as the Stits Skybaby. It cost 40 million dollars ($40,000,000) to build. It had eight engines and weighed 190 tons (171 metric tons). On a test run in Long Beach Harbor in California, it rose 10 feet (3 meters) into the air and flew 1,000 yards (900 meters). It was never flown again.

747 Luxury Liner

What was the heaviest airplane ever flown?

The heaviest airplane ever flown is a 747 that weighs more than 410 tons (about 370 metric tons). That's about as heavy as 82 elephants. Without fuel and equipment it weighs only 160 tons (144 metric tons), about the weight of 32 elephants.

How can a heavy plane stay up in the air?

When a plane is flying, it is being pulled up and down and backward and forward all at the same time. The force of "gravity" pulls the plane downward. "Lift" pushes it upward. Lift is the force made by the wings as they cut through the air. The force of "drag" pulls the plane backward, while "thrust" pushes it forward. Jet engines or propellers give thrust. A heavy plane in steady flight stays in the air for two reasons. The thrust from its engines or propellers equals the drag force. And the lift made by its wings equals the force of gravity on the plane (its weight).

What are the most important parts of an airplane?

An airplane has three main parts. They are the wings, the tail assembly, and the body. The body is called the fuselage (FYOO-suh-lij).

The wings lift the airplane into the sky. Ailerons (AY-luh-ronz) are the flaps on the wings that keep the plane in a curved path during turns. Other flaps on the wings give the plane stronger lift at the slower speeds of takeoff and landing.

The tail assembly keeps the plane steady. The rudder is part of the tail assembly. The pilot can swing the rudder to the right or to the left. When it swings to the right, the front of the plane moves to the right. When it swings to the left, the front of the plane moves to the left.

The fin is another part of the tail assembly. The fin keeps the plane steady in forward flight.

The stabilizer is also part of the tail assembly. The stabilizer keeps the airplane from wobbling up and down in the air. Tail parts, called elevators, that are connected to the stabilizer help the plane go up and down when the plane takes off and lands.

The body is where the passengers and freight are carried.

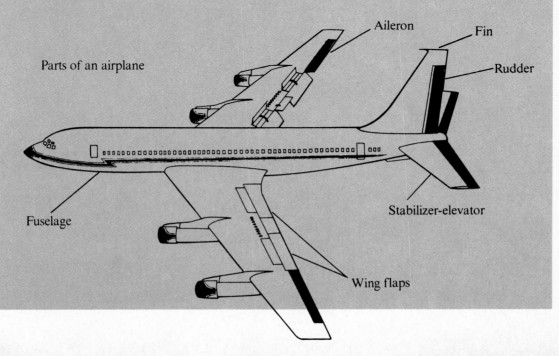

Parts of an airplane

Aileron

Fin

Rudder

Fuselage

Stabilizer-elevator

Wing flaps

How can a plane fly upside down?

A plane can fly upside down because the same forces—lift, drag, thrust, and gravity—that pull on a right-side-up plane also pull on an upside-down plane. The only force that may not be strong in an upside-down plane is lift—the force made by the wings as they cut through the air. As long as the wings have enough lift in the upside-down position, the plane will stay in the air.

But first, the ailerons—movable flaps near the tips of the wings—must turn the plane over. By moving the ailerons with a wheel or a control stick, the pilot can roll the plane over until it is moving along upside down.

What is an automatic pilot?

An automatic pilot is a set of instruments that flies the plane without any help from the human pilot. Perhaps the person flying the plane is busy. Or maybe the weather is bad. The pilot is not able to see clearly because of heavy rain, snow, or fog. Then the pilot may decide to use electronic equipment to fly the plane. The automatic pilot can keep the plane flying in a certain direction. It can keep the plane flying at a particular height in the sky. The automatic pilot can fly the plane more perfectly than a person can.

Someday flight may become completely automatic. Perhaps computers, not people, will guide airplanes through an entire flight.

What is a prop plane?

The "prop" in "prop plane" is short for propeller. A prop plane has blades in the front that spin around. These blades make up the propeller. The propeller helps to move the airplane forward.

How fast can a prop plane fly?

The speed of a prop plane depends upon the size of the plane and how many engines it has. A single-engine, six-passenger plane may reach a speed of 180 miles (288 kilometers) per hour. The fastest prop plane ever built was an experimental Navy model. It was never manufactured for use. This plane reached a top speed of 670 miles (1,072 kilometers) an hour.

Crop spraying plane

125

What is a jet plane?

A jet plane is an aircraft that has jet engines. When fuel is burned in a jet engine, it gives off hot gases. The gases shoot out of the back of the engine in a stream, called a jet. The stream rushing out toward the rear makes the plane move forward. This forward force is called "thrust." A toy balloon filled with air shows how this works. If you suddenly let go of the stem of the balloon, the balloon will zip away. Air rushes from the stem in one direction, pushing the balloon in the other direction—just like the jet plane.

How fast can a jet plane go?

One jet reached a speed of more than 2,193 miles (3,509 kilometers) an hour. But most jets can't go that fast. A plane with two jet engines can go about 560 miles (896 kilometers) an hour. Some jets with four engines can fly faster than 1,000 miles (1,600 kilometers) an hour.

HOW MUCH OF THIS DO I HAVE TO KNOW TO QUALIFY AS A MEMBER OF THE "JET SET?"

Jet engine

Hot gases shoot out the back.

Air stream comes in the front.

Air is mixed with fuel and burned.

What is a "sonic boom"?

A sonic boom is the noise made by a supersonic airplane. Supersonic means faster than the speed of sound traveling through air—about 1,100 feet (330 meters) a second. When a plane is flying, waves of air build up in front of it. When a plane flies faster than the speed of sound, the waves become cone-shaped. The plane is inside the pointed tip of the cone. A cone-shaped air wave is called a shock wave. When the cone sweeps over the ground, the shock wave makes a loud noise or boom. This is called sonic boom. It can break windows and crack walls. And, over a period of time, such loud noise can damage your ears.

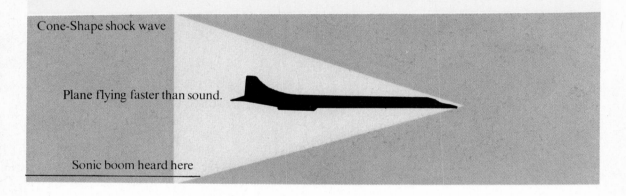

Cone-Shape shock wave

Plane flying faster than sound.

Sonic boom heard here

What is the SST?

SST stands for supersonic transport. SSTs fly faster than the speed of sound. Most planes don't fly nearly that fast. The Russian Tu-144 and the French and British Concordes are supersonic planes. The Concorde flies at about 1,019 miles (about 1,630 kilometers) an hour. A Boeing 747, which is not supersonic, flies at about 595 miles (952 kilometers) an hour.

The SST is shaped like a dart. The wings are thin and swept back. When planes fly at supersonic speeds, air pressure against the fast-moving plane becomes very strong. The SST's nose comes to a sharp point so that the plane can cut through the hard pressure of the air.

A Concorde

What are the newer planes like?

Some of the newer planes are shaped differently from older airplanes. The tail assembly of a plane is usually behind the wings. But a new plane called the Avro Vulcan has a tail assembly that lines up with the wings. It does not extend behind them. The Avro Vulcan is shaped like a triangle. Each wing forms one point of the triangle. The plane's nose forms the third point.

A plane called the Northrop YB-49 has no tail assembly at all. It doesn't have a body either. The passengers, the pilot, and the crew sit inside the wings. The windows are at the edge of the wings so people can look out. The plane is very thick in the middle. The tips of the wings are swept back. The large wings do the work of the tail assembly. They keep the plane steady.

The HL-10 is a wingless plane. It flies by rocket power. It travels at a speed of 610 miles (976 kilometers) an hour as it climbs in the air. When it reaches flying height, the HL-10 moves forward at 1,200 miles (1,920 kilometers) an hour.

The "YB-49," jet-propelled version of the Northrop Flying Wing

Some new planes can fly at 3,600 miles (5,760 kilometers) an hour—about six times the speed of sound!

In what ways are planes used today?

Small planes are used to check telephone lines and pipelines. They're used by photographers who want to take pictures from the sky. Flight instructors use light planes for flying lessons.

Airplanes are used by the armed forces. Some planes are big enough to carry tanks and large numbers of soldiers. Most military planes are bombers or fighter planes that are designed for sky battles.

Farmers use specially built planes to spray their crops against insect pests. These planes have large tanks to store chemicals. A Canadian plane that can suck up water from lakes is used to fight fires.

Some planes are designed for stunt flying and air races. And last, but not least, large airliners carry people and cargo all over the world.

United States Air Force Thunderbirds in formation flight

Who invented the helicopter?

About 500 years ago, a famous artist named Leonardo da Vinci (duh VIN-chee) designed the first helicopter. He drew pictures of it, but never built it. In 1939, Igor Sikorsky (EE-gore sih-CORE-skee) designed the first helicopter that worked. But an autogyro (AW-toe-JIE-row), an airplane with blades on top, was built by Juan de la Cierva (day lah see-AIR-vuh) in 1920. The blades were spun, not by the engine, but by the motion of the air as the plane traveled through it. Unlike our modern helicopter, the autogyro couldn't stay still in the air.

Sikorsky flying an early helicopter.

Why don't helicopters need big airports?

Helicopters can move straight up and down in the air. So they don't need a lot of space to take off and land. The place where they do take off and land is called a heliport. It may be on the ground, the roof of a building, or the deck of a ship.

How can a helicopter go straight up?

Instead of regular wings, a helicopter has three or more wing-like blades mounted on top of it. They are called rotor (ROE-tur) blades. They whirl around in a fast circle. The pressure of the air under the blades becomes greater than the pressure of the air on top. The greater pressure pushes upward on the blades, and the helicopter is lifted into the air. By changing the tilt, or angle, of the blades, the pilot can move the helicopter forward or backward. When the blades are not tilted, the helicopter can stay in one spot.

Is there any plane with wings that can fly straight up?

Yes, the convertiplane can fly straight up and down. It can take off and land like a helicopter. But once it is in the air, it flies like an airplane. Some convertiplanes have rotating blades on top. Those that don't, sometimes work by turning or tilting their wings or engines. Others use a special system of flaps and vanes. Convertiplanes cost more to build than regular airplanes.

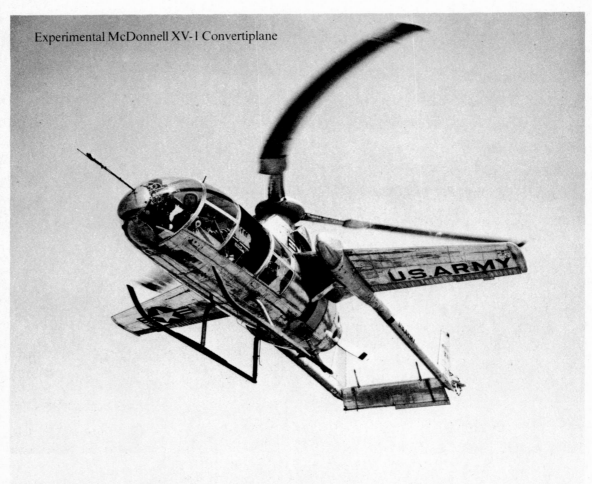

Experimental McDonnell XV-1 Convertiplane

What is an amphibian?

An amphibian (am-FIB-ee-un) is an airplane that can land on ground or on water. The pilot pulls the wheels up in order to land the plane on water. The pilot lowers the wheels for a ground landing. This airplane was named after the animals known as amphibians. Animal amphibians live part of their lives in water and part on land. Frogs, toads, and salamanders are all amphibians.

What is a seaplane?

A seaplane is an airplane that can land and take off on water. It has floats instead of landing wheels.

How do some airplanes write in the sky?

When a metal called titanium (tie-TAY-nee-um) is mixed with chlorine gas, it makes smoke. A skywriting airplane carries this mixture in a tank. The pilot uses the plane like a "pen." He releases the smoke and flies in the pattern of the words he is spelling. The result is big, white letters in the sky.

135

How many scheduled airlines are there in the United States?

There are 35 scheduled airlines. They fly between 690 places around the world. A scheduled airline flies planes every day at fixed times. Non-scheduled airlines make up to ten round-trip flights a month. But they have no fixed time schedules. Feeder airlines are smaller airline companies that make only short flights. They fly between small towns or between small towns and large city airports.

View from a jet approaching a New York airport.

Scheduled airlines in the United States carry more than 200 million passengers a year!

POOR WOODSTOCK... WITH ALL THAT AIR TRAFFIC, HE'S AFRAID THEY MAY BAN THE BIRDS!!

How many airports are there in the United States?

There are about 13,000 airports in the United States. Of these, more than 4,000 are open to the general public. About 8,000 are privately owned and may be used only by members of a club. And more than 400 are military airports, open only to people in the armed forces.

What is the largest airport in the world?

The world's largest airport is the Dallas/Fort Worth Airport in Texas. It extends over an area of 17,500 acres (7,000 hectares). It is about the size of an average small city. When this airport is completed, it will have 9 runways, 13 terminals, and 260 gates. Sixty million passengers will come through the airport every year.

THE LONESOME COWBOY IS FAST BECOMING AN ENDANGERED SPECIES!

! When it opened in 1974, the Dallas/Fort Worth Airport had already cost seven hundred million dollars ($700,000,000)! **!**

What is the busiest airport in the world?

The world's busiest airport is the Chicago International Airport at O'Hare Field. In 1977, about 44 million passengers went through the Chicago International Airport. There were 749,278 takeoffs and landings. Day and night around the clock there was a takeoff or a landing about every 42 seconds.

How long does it take to build an airport?

It takes from 7 to 10 years before an airport is built and ready to handle passengers. Before an airport is built a master plan is prepared. The master plan shows how an airport will look 20 to 30 years in the future.

The airport is built a section at a time, according to the master plan. As soon as a section is completed it is opened to the public.

Why does an airplane need a runway?

An airplane needs a runway to take off and to land. An airplane must race across the ground to gather speed before the lift force is strong enough to raise it off the ground.

Small planes can leave the ground at speeds of only 30–40 miles (48–64 kilometers) an hour. That is slower than cars normally travel on a highway. Heavier planes may have to reach 100 miles (160 kilometers) an hour before they can lift into the air. That is almost twice the speed limit for cars on a highway.

Big airliners need a long runway to gain enough speed to take off. Some runways are more than a mile long. An airplane also needs a long runway to land and slow down to a stop.

What happens to a plane before it is ready to take off?

An airplane is thoroughly checked by the airline's safety crew before it is allowed to leave the airport. A person from the Federal Aviation Administration spot-checks the plane to be sure it is safe. Everything in the airplane must be working correctly. Mechanics who work on it are well trained. They know how to take an engine completely apart. They can put it together again so that it runs perfectly.

A "safety man" checks the weight of the baggage, the passengers, and the cargo. The dispatcher decides the route the pilot will take and how high up he should fly. The weather station tells the pilot what the weather conditions will be like during the flight.

The pilot and the flight crew check the instruments on the control panel. They use a check list. The pilot names an instrument. The co-pilot or flight engineer tests the instrument to be sure it is working right. The pilot starts the engines. He speaks to the control tower by radio. The control tower tells the pilot which runway to use.

What aircraft can go higher than jet planes?

Rockets can go higher than jet planes. Both rockets and jets need oxygen or their fuel won't burn. Jets must get their oxygen from the air. Since there is no air in outer space, they cannot fly there. Rockets contain their own oxygen so they can fly in outer space.

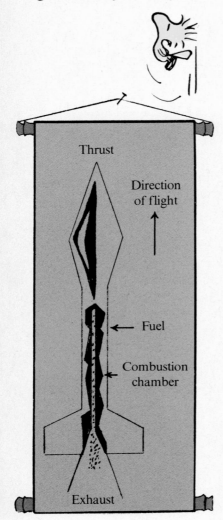

How does a rocket engine work?

A simple rocket engine is a tube closed at one end and open at the other end. It contains fuel and oxygen. The oxygen is needed to burn the fuel. When the fuel burns, it turns into a gas. The hot gas pushes out in all directions inside the rocket tube. It rushes out the open end. Gas rushing out in one direction pushes the rocket in the other direction. In rocket language, this push is called "thrust." The greater the thrust, the faster the rocket picks up speed.

You can see for yourself how a rocket works. Put a garden hose on flat ground. Turn on the water full force. The nozzle of the hose will be pushed backward as the water rushes out.

A rocket engine works much like a jet engine. But the jet engine must take in oxygen from the outside air to burn its fuel. The rocket carries its own oxygen supply.

What was the first rocket sent into space?

A Chinese youth in about the year 1200 put some chemicals in a tube and attached a fuse to it. He lit the fuse and fired the first skyrocket. It was like the rockets we use in Fourth of July fireworks. It could not travel very far.

Robert Goddard, an American scientist, sent up a new kind of rocket in 1926. It traveled as high as a 20-story building. But it wasn't until 1957 that a rocket reached what is called "outer space." That begins about 100 miles (160 kilometers) above the earth. This time the Russians were the successful ones. They sent Sputnik I into orbit around the world.

How fast can a modern rocket go?

Modern rockets are fast travelers. They usually race through space at 18,000–25,000 miles (29,000–40,000 kilometers) an hour. At the fastest of these speeds, you could circle the entire earth in only one hour!

Dr. Robert H. Goddard with an early rocket.

Apollo 15 Saturn V lifting off
to the Moon on July 26, 1971.

Did Charlie Brown and Snoopy ever fly into outer space?

Yes! "Charlie Brown" and "Snoopy" were nicknames for parts of the Apollo 10 spacecraft. The Saturn V rocket lifted Apollo 10 into space.

Astronauts Young, Cernan, and Stafford sat in a part of the spacecraft called Charlie Brown. When they were 69 miles (110 kilometers) above the moon, Cernan and Stafford crawled through a tunnel to another part of the spacecraft. Now they were inside Snoopy.

Snoopy separated from Charlie Brown. Inside Snoopy, Cernan and Stafford came within 9 miles (more than 14 kilometers) of the moon. From there they took some pictures. Then Snoopy rejoined Charlie Brown, which was still flying around the moon. Cernan and Stafford climbed back into Charlie Brown.

Apollo 10 increased its speed. Snoopy was sent to fly around the moon alone. Charlie Brown and the astronauts headed towards Earth for a safe splashdown.

Apollo 10

142

How might people travel 100 years from now?

How does a flying umbrella sound to you? Or maybe you'd prefer a flying belt or a flying car to take you where you want to go. All of these may be possible 100 years from now.

By then a "flying saucer" could become a reality. It might be kept in the sky by streams of air that rush from the saucer-shaped vehicle. It would probably be able to travel through space, too.

Rocket ships powered by nuclear energy will probably be used a lot 100 years from now. These rocket ships would move very fast. They might even be able to reach other planets in only a few days' time.

Space stations in the sky may become as common as train stations are today. And space shuttles might carry you from one space stop to another.

Are flying saucers real?

Many reliable people have reported seeing strange sights in the sky. Some of these people said the objects looked like large saucers. Scientists call flying saucers **U**nidentified **F**lying **O**bjects, or UFOs. Most UFOs have turned out to be either the reflections of lights or natural space objects.

Sometimes clouds are shaped like huge saucers.

Meteors are often thought to be UFOs. Meteors are bright trails made by chunks of metal or stone that enter the earth's atmosphere from outer space. A meteor usually burns up completely as it moves through the air. Any piece that reaches the ground is called a meteorite.

Some UFOs were really fireballs—very bright meteors. Some fireballs explode. Pieces of the fireball may fall to earth. A fireball can look as bright as a star or even as bright as the moon.

Comets have been mistaken for UFOs, too. A comet is a huge mass of frozen gas, ice, and dust. The comet travels around the sun in a definite path. We can see a comet only when it comes near the earth. A comet looks like a fuzzy star with a long tail. Sometimes the tail is millions of miles long.

Some UFOs don't seem to have any explanation. But so far, no one has proven that any of these UFOs were spaceships from other planets.

Index

References to pictures are in *italic type*.